T0334186

Beyond Think-Pair-Share

This book shows you how to teach K-12 students to work in pairs and groups more effectively, so that true collaboration can happen in the classroom. Coming from their experience in social work and classroom teaching, Christina M. Krantz and Laura Gullette Smith explain the problems that can occur with traditional Think-Pair-Share models and offer refreshing solutions. They provide practical strategies to help students build collegial peer relationships, learn to share tasks, and hold deeper discussions. Each chapter offers useful strategies that you can implement immediately. This book includes an invaluable appendix of resources that the authors share when leading workshops, as well as rubrics, agendas, and classroom tools designed with the strategies covered in each chapter in mind.

Christina M. Krantz is an educational consultant and certified social worker at Central Kentucky Educational Cooperative with ten years of educational experience. Areas of expertise include mental health, building relationships, resilience, trauma-informed care, and post-secondary transition for students with disabilities. Follow her on social media at @ChristinaK1978 (Twitter) and christina_krantz (Instagram).

Laura Gullette Smith is an instructional consultant at Central Kentucky Educational Cooperative with 24 years in the field of education that include K-5 classroom experience and instructional coaching, as well as consulting and training school districts in PreK-12 in Central Kentucky. Follow her on social media at @lgullsmith (Twitter) and @llgull (Instagram).

Other Eye On Education Books

Available from Routledge
www.routledge.com/eyeoneducation

**Managing Classroom Assessment to
Enhance Student Learning**
Nicole Barnes and Helenrose Fives

**What Great Teachers Do Differently: Nineteen Things
That Matter Most**
Todd Whitaker

**Math Running Records in Action: A Framework
for Assessing Basic Fact Fluency in Grades K-5**
Dr. Nicki Newton

**The Genius Hour Guidebook: Fostering Passion,
Wonder, and Inquiry in the Classroom, 2nd Edition**
Denise Krebs and Gallit Zvi

**Evaluating the K–12 Literacy Curriculum: A Step
by Step Guide for Auditing Programs,
Materials, and Instructional Approaches**
Colleen Pennell

Essential Truths for Teachers
Danny Steele and Todd Whitaker

**From Texting to Teaching: Grammar Instruction
in a Digital Age**
Jeremy Hyler and Troy Hicks

**Active Literacy Across the Curriculum: Connecting Print
Literacy with Digital, Media, and Global Competence, K–12**
Heidi Hayes Jacobs

Beyond
Think-Pair-Share

A Quick Guide to Effective Collaboration

Christina M. Krantz and Laura Gullette Smith

Routledge
Taylor & Francis Group

NEW YORK AND LONDON

First published 2021
by Routledge
52 Vanderbilt Avenue, New York, NY 10017

and by Routledge
2 Park Square, Milton Park, Abingdon, Oxon OX14 4RN

Routledge is an imprint of the Taylor & Francis Group, an informa business

© 2021 Taylor & Francis

The right of Christina M. Krantz and Laura Gullette Smith to be identified as authors of this work has been asserted by them in accordance with sections 77 and 78 of the Copyright, Designs and Patents Act 1988.

All rights reserved. No part of this book may be reprinted or reproduced or utilized in any form or by any electronic, mechanical, or other means, now known or hereafter invented, including photocopying and recording, or in any information storage or retrieval system, without permission in writing from the publishers.

Trademark notice: Product or corporate names may be trademarks or registered trademarks, and are used only for identification and explanation without intent to infringe.

Library of Congress Cataloging-in-Publication Data
Names: Krantz, Christina M., author. | Smith, Laura Gullette, author.
Title: Beyond think-pair-share : a quick guide to effective collaboration / Christina M. Krantz and Laura Gullette Smith.
Description: New York, NY : Routledge, 2021. |
Includes bibliographical references.
Identifiers: LCCN 2020019980 (print) | LCCN 2020019981 (ebook) |
ISBN 9780367374556 (hardback) | ISBN 9780367374549 (paperback) |
ISBN 9780429354595 (ebook)
Subjects: LCSH: Group work in education. |
Interpersonal communication–Study and teaching. |
Interaction analysis in education. | Classroom environment.
Classification: LCC LB1032 .K65 2021 (print) |
LCC LB1032 (ebook) | DDC 371.39/5–dc23
LC record available at https://lccn.loc.gov/2020019980
LC ebook record available at https://lccn.loc.gov/2020019981

ISBN: 978-0-367-37455-6 (hbk)
ISBN: 978-0-367-37454-9 (pbk)
ISBN: 978-0-429-35459-5 (ebk)

Typeset in Palatino
by Newgen Publishing UK

To Taylor and Connor
Be a leader. Make good choices. I love you.

To Matt
For picking up the slack so I can realize my dreams.

To David
I dedicate this book to you for supporting my endeavors and being a part of developing relationships with my students and their families.

To Aiden
May you develop relationships that foster a love for learning like your LaLa.

Contents

Introduction

What happens when a certified social worker and an experienced teacher become colleagues at a regional special education cooperative? We combine our experience and knowledge to design training sessions that address social-emotional learning and relationship building to increase student engagement and academic achievement. We're both certified Ruby Payne trainers in "A Framework in Understanding Poverty" and "Emotional Poverty." We strive to provide a foundational understanding of the implications of students living in poverty or experiencing trauma and identify strategies for building classroom relationships. We provide instructional methods that foster engagement and collaboration to help participants attending our sessions develop a toolbox of resources and easy-to-implement strategies to promote classroom success for all students.

In our state in 2019, there were over 10,000 children in foster care (KVC, 2020). These children show up in our classrooms and in our communities. Our educators need help to serve these students and practical strategies to reach them. This book is actually based on training that we developed in response to the growing numbers of children experiencing traumatic events and poverty. It's based on the premise that leveraging student-to-teacher and peer-to-peer relationships for student engagement and collaboration can increase positive outcomes for all of our students. We've received a lot of positive feedback on the training and have presented it at both state and national conferences.

Laura had the opportunity to meet with Dr. Nicki Newton at the ASCD conference and told her about this "Beyond Think-Pair-Share" training and the feedback we had received. Dr. Newton said we should write a book about that. So, after a quick introduction to a publishing representative in the exhibit hall and a few phone calls later – we did just that! We're excited to be able to share these strategies with a wider audience.

With ten years of experience as a social worker, Christina has a passion for teaching skills and strategies to effectively help students from diverse backgrounds. Christina is passionate about giving a voice to those who are voiceless, whether they are affected by trauma, poverty, or other life circumstances. Many of the ideas shared in this book provide opportunities for students to experience equity and the opportunity for voice in the classroom.

A total of 24 years of classroom teaching, coaching, and training has provided Laura with notable experiences of building relationships with not only students and their families, but fellow teachers and colleagues as well. She firmly believes that positive classroom relationships are the key to ensuring academic success, especially for diverse populations and struggling learners. This belief is echoed throughout the book in the strategies shared.

We know how trying being an educator can be. We have the privilege of working with teachers and other school staff every day to create better outcomes for some of our most vulnerable students. It is our sincerest hope that this book will provide you with a practical tool that provides not only the research behind why relationships and collaborative work are important, but also a how-to guide with strategies to scaffold and support implementation.

Reference

KVC. (2020, February 10). *How many children are in foster care?* Retrieved February 13, 2020, from https://kentucky.kvc.org/2019/05/06/how-many-children-are-in-foster-care/

Acknowledgements

Our Acknowledgements

We would like to thank math expert and author Dr. Nicki Newton for planting the seed that our "Building Relationships" content should be shared with a wider audience through writing a book.

Thanks to Lauren Davis and Emily Dombrovskaya at Taylor & Francis for providing us with encouragement and direction on this new project.

We would like to thank our CKEC family for their encouragement, support, and camaraderie. We would also like to acknowledge educators throughout the central Kentucky region for attending our sessions and providing positive feedback.

Amy Martin – for providing valuable insight into her awesome middle-school classroom!

Christina's Acknowledgements

A huge thank you to my children and husband for their support, love, and for being my biggest fans. To my mom, my brother, Uncle Shawn, and Aunt Carolyn for always being there and believing me even when I wasn't so sure myself. Amy M. for all of your help, support, and love from way back in the day. Finally, to my circle of kick-butt friends, new and old. You all are the absolute best and I'm so grateful that you always keep it real and provide words of encouragement and motivation.

Laura's Acknowledgements

I first want to acknowledge my parents and my Nan for always supporting and encouraging me, when growing up and still as an adult today. To them, David, and the rest of my family, please know that I love you beyond measure and that you are appreciated. To my tribe that I'm lucky to call my friends: you will never know what your friendship and support mean to us. I would also like to thank a handful of special people that have served as mentors, in one way or another, for providing me with leadership opportunities to grow and become the educator I am today. I certainly can't forget to acknowledge my Ruby for being a perfect example of how human–pet relationships foster well-being and happiness.

1

How Do You Do It? Building Connections *with* Students

There is no denying the power of human connection. As human service professionals, we see the evidence of its importance every day. We see it in the happy, smiling faces of our students. We see it in how our students interact with each other. We see it in how our colleagues talk with one another. We can see evidence of the power of human connection literally just about everywhere. Unfortunately, we also see the devastating effects of the lack of human connection – in the news, on social media, and sadly, sometimes even in our classrooms.

Educators are being tasked with more and more responsibilities every day and, often, to do more with less. One of the biggest bang-for-your-buck strategies is cultivating positive and appropriate relationships with your students. We can all name a teacher from our past who made going to school worth it; a teacher for whom we would work just a little harder. When we've asked others about what made that teacher different, we get very similar responses: the teacher made class fun; they knew my name; they took an interest in me. These are all seemingly simple gestures that have a lifelong, lasting impact.

So, just how important are relationships in education? Again, we see the evidence every day in our schools. Just in case that's not enough, numerous studies have shown the positive effects of the relational aspects of teaching. Students who have connections to school do better academically and have more academic resilience (Battistich, Schaps, & Wilson, 2004; Birch & Ladd, 1997; Curby, Rimm-Kaufman, & Ponitz, 2009; Ewing & Taylor, 2009; Hamre & Pianta, 2001; Rudasill, Reio, Stipanovic, & Taylor, 2010).

Research also shows that students who have positive school relationships are less likely to engage in all of those risky behaviors that schools have been tasked with eliminating. A reduction was noted in risky behaviors like smoking, drinking, drug use, violence, and early sexual activity (Blum, 2005).

Relationships aren't just beneficial for students. Teachers benefit from them also. Teachers who have positive relationships with students are likely to be less stressed (Gregory, Allen, Mikami, Hafen, & Pianta, 2013) and are more likely to have high-achieving classrooms (Hamre & Pianta, 2006). Classroom climates will change as a result of teacher–student relationships. As students begin to feel more connected to their teacher, they will also begin to feel more connected to their fellow students. This results in a classroom environment where students feel safe and supported to engage in group work and to take risks in their learning.

Now, we know that sometimes developing relationships takes time. It can be difficult and exhausting. Some students are more resistant than others. We can all think of a student with whom we have worked who had no desire to connect with us, no matter what trick or strategy we used. Thankfully, the majority of our students come to school already having some experience with positive and caring relationships. This gives them a head start in school and with learning. Sadly, this is not the case for all of our students. What about the students who come to school with little to no experience of positive relationships? Studies show that the brain is negatively affected by the lack of positive relationships. Students who have negative or inconsistent experiences with relationships don't have as many neural pathways in their brains (Child Welfare Gateway, 2015). This lack of neural connections makes it difficult to learn and develop positive relationships. The good news is that we, as adults, can make a positive difference in the lives of these students. It may not be easy or quick and it may be heartbreaking at times. Through the power of positive relationships, you can literally alter the makeup of someone's brain! How cool is that?

Do you want to improve your classroom climate? Positive student–teacher relationships can help with that too! A study conducted by Donohue, Perry, and Weinstein (2003) found that when first-grade teachers had caring attitudes toward their students, those students were more likely to be accepted by other students. There is also research to support that students who struggle with aggression, but who have positive relationships with teachers, are more likely to be accepted by their classmates (Hughes, Cavell, & Wilson, 2001).

Establishing Boundaries

Whenever we talk about developing and establishing relationships, we get asked about boundaries. It seems like every couple of months, news or social media are sharing stories about inappropriate student–teacher relationships. Boundaries are absolutely necessary in any relationship, not just those that occur between students and teachers. Boundaries help to keep us safe professionally and personally. Here are some guidelines to establishing boundaries that we always share with our participants.

◆ Boundaries should always be established at the beginning of a relationship. We've all been in situations where a certain behavior was acceptable one day and then, a few days, weeks, or months later, it wasn't. Setting clear limits from the start helps to prevent confusion.

◆ Talk about your responsibilities. Establish what you will and won't do, as well as what you can and can't do. We know some students will attempt to take advantage of your relationship by trying to get tardy notes to class or not turning in assignments on time. Letting them know ahead of time that your relationship is not a free pass for misbehavior or special treatment will help. If you find yourself saying you will do it "just this once," you are more than likely violating a boundary.

◆ Establish the limits of confidentiality. It's vital for students to know that what they say to you will be kept confidential. It is equally important for them to know that there are limits to confidentiality. No, you will not tell everyone in the building that they like someone or that they still sleep with a night light. But you will have to tell someone if they disclose information that might sound like abuse or neglect, or that sounds like it could be harmful to self or others; you are mandated to share that information with others. Another note about the limits of confidentiality: It is not a two-way street where students are concerned. While we can and should expect students to hold information within the confines of confidentiality, that doesn't mean that they will. If you decide to share a particularly juicy tidbit of information about yourself with a student, you can fully expect that it will have circulated around the building by lunch. Which brings us to our next point.

◆ Decide how much information you are willing to share with your students. Students have an uncanny ability to catch us completely off guard with questions – often personal in nature. The last thing you want is to be leading a class discussion when a student asks if you drank before you were of legal age, or if you had premarital sex, or why you aren't married – and not have any idea on how you are going to respond. It's best to be prepared ahead of time and know how much and what topics you are willing to divulge.

◆ Know what your district and school policies, procedures, and practices are when it comes to communicating with students. Does your district have a social media policy? What about communication with personal electronic devices? Are you allowed to text students? Send emails? Technology can create some sticky situations for teachers.

♦ Consistency is key. Maintaining boundaries works best when you stick to them all of the time. When we are tired, stressed, or hungry – or even happy – we may be less likely to remember our boundaries and may let things slide. Know your limits and stick to them.

♦ Whoever has the stricter boundary, gets to set the boundary. We have found that the best way to illustrate this is with an example. Christina is known around the office as a non-hugger. She'll happily hug her children, and other family members, and that's about it. Nearly everyone else in the office is pro-hug. Christina gets to establish the boundary for hugging because she has the stricter boundary. The same standard goes into effect when working with students as well. At times, their boundaries may be stricter than yours and vice versa.

♦ Communicate your boundaries. Be upfront with people about your boundaries. Don't be embarrassed about taking steps to protect yourself. Christina recently established some boundaries around technology, specifically responding to text messages and emails after work hours. Great idea, right? The only problem? She completely forgot to tell her colleagues that she would no longer be responding to work-related texts and emails after 4:00 p.m. Thankfully, a quick explanation cleared things up when she was asked about it. So, whether your boundary is around limiting technology use, or your policy on turning in late assignments, be sure to communicate it with those who are likely to be affected by it (colleagues, your students, and their families).

Respecting boundaries is vital in establishing and maintaining relationships. It can sometimes seem like having boundaries is at odds with the relational aspects of teaching. Having and maintaining boundaries provides protection for both students and teachers. When working with students affected by trauma or poverty, and students receiving special education services, you may need to be explicit with stating your boundaries. Be prepared to remind students about your boundaries and your limits more often in the beginning. Once students become more familiar with your limits, they should need fewer reminders. Strategies will be shared later in this chapter on how to connect with students while still maintaining boundaries.

Button Pushers

We all have experience with students, colleagues, and even family members who know exactly what to do or say to push us over the edge. It often happens quickly and without us really knowing it. One minute you are calm and collected, the next you are telling the student to leave the class and go to the office. In the world of trauma-informed care, these behaviors or words are called triggers because they set off an automatic reaction. Being aware of what causes us to have an automatic reaction, whether it be whining, disrespect, or bad grammar, can help us be more effective educators. It's also possible that a boundary violation has taken place. If you are mindful about what behaviors are going to push your buttons, you can find strategies to help you stay calm when they occur. Strategies may include:

- ◆ Taking a deep breath. Actually, taking three deep breaths. We know that having our students take a deep breath can help them to regulate their emotions. It's no different for adults. It can help regulate your body's stress response. Having the student join you in taking some deep breaths will benefit them also.
- ◆ Counting to ten (or even longer if possible). Another strategy to help lower your body's stress response is by taking a quick time out. Some studies show that when angry, IQ can drop between 10 and 15 points (Nadler, 2011). This is partly because your stress-response system has been activated. Taking a few seconds can help get your body's stress response back to center and can give your IQ a chance to return to normal. It also gives you an opportunity to create an appropriate response to what is happening around you.

◆ Changing your stance. At times, a subtle shift in your body placement can help you regain your composure. It could be as subtle as tilting your head to the left or taking a small step back. This can help signal to your brain that there is no threat and you can deactivate your stress response.

◆ Getting a drink of water. Cortisol is a stress hormone that is released when your body's stress-response system is activated. Water has been shown to reduce the amount of cortisol in your system (Nowak, 2017).

◆ Reframing what is happening. Sometimes we get so caught up in confrontations or other situations with our students that we automatically see the behavior from a deficit-based model. What if we flipped it and looked at the situation from a strengths-based perspective? What if you were able to see a student's defiance as determination? Their disruptive behavior as an eagerness to share? Their non-participation as being thoughtful?

◆ Considering student boundaries. We've already discussed the possibility of boundary violations occurring when your buttons get pushed; the same could be true for your students. If a student is being confrontational, it's possible there's been a boundary violation. Sometimes, students don't even realize that this has happened. If we did not violate a boundary, it's possible that we've unknowingly triggered the student's flight, fight, or freeze response. When time permits, consider the situation. What happened before the incident began? Is it possible that something was said or done to cause embarrassment for the student? Even when inadvertent, embarrassment or humiliation can be a trigger for some students. This is when really knowing your students and their backgrounds can be helpful. Sometimes, considering things from a student's perspective can help us realize there's more to the situation.

So, we've discussed the importance of relationships. And now comes the fun part: Actually building relationships with students.

So, how do you do it? Let's look at some simple, straightforward strategies to use to build relationships with students, regardless of their age. While in the process of getting to know your students, you will need to actively model how to get to know others, pro-social skills, and relationships. Some of our students don't see positive relationships modeled at home. We will have to be explicit in what we expect from our students. We will need to model relationship-building skills with everyone in our classroom. This includes paraeducators, instructional assistants, co-teachers, and anyone else who comes into your classroom.

When getting to know students who may be trauma affected or have a background of poverty, you may need to practice radical patience. It is possible these students have little, if any, experience with positive relationships. Even students not affected by adverse circumstances may not have a lot of experience with positive relationships. Be prepared for it to take longer than expected – maybe even all year. They may try to push you away or try to make you quit. The way to get these students to connect and trust is through being consistent and genuine.

Rapport

You must first begin by establishing a rapport with your students. Rapport is one of those ideas that can be difficult to explain, but we know it when we see it. The best and easiest explanation is that rapport is a connection between two people. You can feel a sense of rapport with your students from the very first day of school. Establishing rapport in classrooms can be daunting given the demands of teaching. Creating a rapport with your students is one of the easiest ways to see results in your classroom. It isn't necessarily part of the core content curriculum. Once rapport is established, it'll pay off in dividends. It results in increased instructional time, increased time on task, and increased student engagement (Frisby & Martin, 2010).

Establishing and maintaining rapport with some students, such as those who may have been affected by trauma, can be trying. At times it may seem like there is nothing you can do and no way to reach them or any way to connect. The best advice we can give for dealing with the hard-to-reach students is to stick with it. Be consistent and reliable and stable. These students are in great need of consistency and stability. Providing that stability and consistency in your classroom is how you will manage to reach those students. They don't have time for people who do not follow through on what they say they are going to do.

When starting out in education, you may have heard the advice of not smiling at your students until after winter break. We are all for setting boundaries and expectations from the beginning, but not smiling? It doesn't make any sense! Not smiling at your students may achieve compliance, but it won't get you student engagement. One of the quickest and easiest ways to establish rapport with students is to smile at them! We aren't advocating for you to walk around grinning like a Cheshire Cat all day, every day. That would be creepy and students (especially older students) will call you out for not being authentic. We are saying that genuine smiles make students feel welcome and can help to build trust. This strategy also goes a long way in establishing rapport with other faculty and staff members in the building too.

Another one of the most simple and effective things you can do to connect with a student is to use their preferred name when speaking with them. Not only should you use their preferred name, you should learn how to say it correctly (McLaughlin, 2017). A name is a part of your student's story. It holds meaning and value to them. Don't give your student a nickname just because you haven't been able to pronounce their name. Doing so may take away a part of the student's identity (Khan-Baker, 2016).

Professional sales-people excel at using people's names almost excessively at times. It sounds so simple. Unfortunately, many of our students don't hear their names used in positive statements often enough. Call on students by name whenever possible. Greet students by name when you see them, both inside and outside of the classroom. Calling students by their names creates a sense of trust and helps students to feel respected and seen.

So, you've established some rapport with your students. Now what? Smiling and using your students' names can get you only so far. Now you need some strategies to get to know your students. These types of activities generally take place at the start of the school year. Sometimes it's asking them to stand up and tell us about themselves. Other times it's in the form of "all about me" bags where students are invited to put three to five items that show their interests, hobbies, or talents into a brown bag. Both achieve the same outcome. You and the students in your class will learn some basic information about each other.

Student Expectations

At the start of every school year or semester, we spend time teaching our students the expectations and rules for our class-room and our school. Have you ever considered asking your students what they need to be successful or engaged in your classroom? At times, students are taken by surprise when asked this question. It's important for students to feel they can be candid with their answers. This strategy does require some set up as it's important for students to feel safe enough to be honest with their responses. Assuring students that all responses will be reviewed and kept confidential will be key in getting feedback. It's also important to share how you plan on using the responses. Will you use some of their answers to assist in creating lesson plans? To help structure the class or school day? To provide incentives? It's not enough to have students share with you what they need to be successful if you aren't going to implement at least some of their suggestions. Be upfront about the limitations you may have in implementing their suggestions. If your school has strict pol-icies against certain things (e.g. having snacks in the classroom or technology use), it's important to be clear that those will not be violated, but there may be other suggestions that you could implement.

For middle-school and high-school students, you may want to give this as a homework assignment so that students have

Sentence Starters for Student Expectations for the Classroom

1. I like to learn by_____.
2. I learn best when _____.
3. My favorite way to learn is _____.
4. I don't like when my teacher asks me to _____.
5. _____helps me pay more attention.
6. I don't like to learn by _____.
7. My least favorite way to learn is _____.

FIGURE 1.1
Sentence Starter Examples for Sharing Student Expectations

an opportunity to be thoughtful in their responses. Younger students, students affected by trauma, or those who receive special education services may benefit from doing this as a small-group activity, or by having some sentence starters. See Figure 1.1 for some examples.

Giving students the opportunities to share with you how they learn best can help create a climate where students feel valued, heard, and respected. It can also give valuable insight into preferred learning styles, hopes the students have for your class, and potential barriers to learning. The idea of student expectations will be revisited in Chapter 3 as it pertains specifically to student behavior.

Suggestion Box

Over the course of the year students may want to share information with you, but they may not feel comfortable sharing them face to face. A suggestion box is one way where you can provide an opportunity for student voice and input. It can be as simple as a box on your desk. Make sure that the box is secure enough so that students can't open it. You'll need to introduce the process and the parameters for leaving a suggestion. See Figure 1.2 for an example of a secondary suggestion form and Figure 1.3 for an example of an elementary suggestion form.

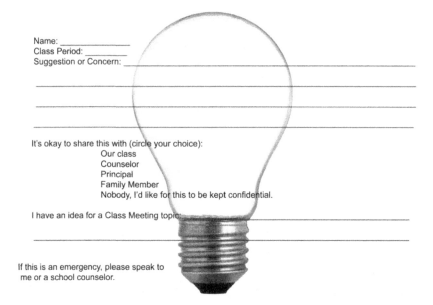

FIGURE 1.2
Example of a Secondary Suggestion Form

FIGURE 1.3
Example of an Elementary Suggestion Form

Considerations that you may want to include in this process:

◆ Where will the suggestion box be kept? Will it be kept some other place after school hours and when school is not in session?

◆ How do students submit a suggestion? Is it a paper-and-pencil form? Is it an online survey such as a Google Form or a JotForm? You may also want to address whether or not students have to include their name on the form. It's perfectly acceptable for the name to be optional. A student's decision to include their name may be determined by what type of response the student would like.

◆ How will you keep the suggestions safe? If using a physical container, does it lock? If using a technology platform, are the responses password protected? Who else will see the suggestions and concerns that are submitted?

◆ How often will the suggestion box be checked?

◆ What will you do with the responses? How will the suggestions and concerns be addressed?

◆ What are topics, suggestions, or concerns that should NOT be shared through the suggestion box? These could include emergent situations – disclosing abuse, neglect, and harm to self and others.

Biopoems

Biopoems are not a new strategy for educators or other helping professionals. They are another excellent way to get a lot of data about students. Biopoems give great insight into how and what our students think about themselves. These are generally best used once you've already established rapport with your students and have established your classroom as a safe, trusting space. Biopoems follow a simple structure and generally do not rhyme. Figure 1.4 shows the structure for the biopoem that we use. Other structures can be found by searching for biopoems on your favorite search engine. Some changes we've made include the phrasing on Line 4, for the student to list things they used to fear,

Biopoem

Line 1: First name
Line 2: Four relationships you value
Line 3: Three words others would use to describe you
Line 4: Three things you fear or used to fear
Line 5: Three things you don't believe or believe in
Line 6: Four things you do believe or believe in
Line 7: Three hopes or dreams you have
Line 8: Four words you'd use to describe yourself
Line 9: Three things you want others to say about you when you're gone
Line 10: Resident of or citizen of
Line 11: Last name

FIGURE 1.4
Possible Biopoem Structure

although some students will never feel comfortable admitting to having fears as it may expose some vulnerabilities.

This strategy provides a goldmine of student information. It provides information on how the student sees themselves, how they want others to see them, and their beliefs. From the very start of the biopoem, you have an opportunity to learn about connections that the student values. You may learn that their most valued relationships are with coaches, or extended family, or even adults in your building. Line 3 gives you information on how a student feels others perceive them. If on Line 7 the student says they hope to change the world, it gives you an opening to ask them to expand on their thinking ("In what ways would you like to change the world?"). This strategy can be done at any grade level. See Figure 1.5 for an elementary school example.

It's acceptable to invite students to share their biopoems with the class. If students choose to share their work with the class, it's vital to celebrate their willingness to share. Sharing something so personal could create feelings of vulnerability in some students. We want to make sure that students are supported while sharing their biopoems. Adding an incentive for reading their work out loud to the class could encourage students to share.

FIGURE 1.5
A Third Grader's Biopoem

A word of caution: It is not for us to disagree with the words and descriptors that our students choose to use. It's important to remember that this biopoem is the perception of the student and it's how they see themselves. If our students write negative descriptors that we disagree with, we should see that as an opportunity to help students see themselves in a different light. The "Finding Hidden Strengths" strategy described below can help with this as well.

If you are having difficulty engaging some students with this strategy because they are reluctant (which is perfectly acceptable because of boundaries), or you don't think your class is ready, you may want to introduce biopoems first, as they relate to content. Literary figures, historical figures, or even scientists and mathematicians are all good options to cite to introduce the idea of biopoems.

Finding Hidden Strengths

Everyone, regardless of circumstances, has strengths. Not all strengths are obvious, and we may need to look a little closer. Enter a strategy we like to call "Finding Hidden Strengths." It follows the strengths-based perspective in social work (Hammond & Zimmerman, n.d.). Reframing strengths takes practice and can feel a little awkward at first. In the beginning you will have to be intentional, especially with those students with whom you struggle. We'll use an example to help. As you read the description of the student Olivia, think about what her strengths are.

Olivia

Olivia is a 17-year-old junior. She moved to your school ready to start the spring semester. Over time, you learned that she has attended three elementary schools, two middle schools, and now two high schools. Olivia has already made a small group of friends. Her friendship group is diverse and includes students from all of the different subgroups at your school. Olivia turns in all of her work on time and does well in your AP English class. At times, Olivia seems bored and even a little annoyed with her fellow classmates when they act silly and get off task. The only time you've seen Olivia get angry is when someone bad mouths her younger brother.

What strengths did you find for Olivia? Olivia possesses several hidden strengths. Moving and having to change school numerous times has helped her to be adaptable and resilient. The small group of friends suggests that she feels quality over quantity. Her diverse friendship group also suggests that she is accepting of others. She seems to care about school, as she does well in class and turns in her work on time. Her annoyance with fellow students when they act silly or off task suggests that Olivia is mature for her age. She values her family and is protective of those she cares about. Now, let's use the hidden strengths strategy with a younger student, Alex.

Alex

Alex is a seven-year-old student in your second-grade class. He tends to be quiet in class. At recess he likes to play with the other students so long as they are playing a game he likes. When he doesn't want to play with the other students, he is happy to do something else. Alex tries really hard in school and is quick to offer answers to your questions. He sometimes gets into trouble for blurting out. Alex receives intervention services in both reading and math. The intervention teacher is pleased with how much growth they have seen in him.

What strengths did you find for Alex? Alex is sociable and also has the confidence and strong sense of self as suggested by his ability to play with peers or alone. This also suggests that he is adaptable. Alex is eager to learn and has the confidence to participate in class. The fact that Alex gets into trouble for blurting out shows that he's passionate about sharing his knowledge with others. Receiving additional intervention help and the intervention teacher being pleased with his growth show that Alex is resilient and is able to persevere.

The ability to reframe personality traits or behaviors is a valuable skill. It is beneficial nearly any time you are working with people. Using a strengths-based perspective doesn't mean that everything will always be sunshine and rainbows. Sometimes there will be situations that will be difficult to reframe, such as aggression or blatant disrespect.

Focusing on strengths is incredibly powerful, especially for students who may have a long history of being seen through a deficit lens. These include trauma-affected students, students from poverty, and students who receive special education services.

We have found that when we operate from a strengths-based perspective, we are more likely to give students the benefit of the doubt and less likely to have kneejerk reactions to their behaviors. A strengths-based perspective can change how we view our students and how students view themselves. We know that students are going to do more of the behaviors that people pay attention to; then why wouldn't we focus on strengths?

Warm Demander

One comment that we get often is that if you have a strong connection to students, they will walk all over you and you can't hold them accountable. While this may be true for some teachers and students, it is not for the majority. For most educators, quite the opposite is true. You can have a connection and rapport with your students, have high expectations of them, and hold them accountable at the same time. This is referred to as being a "warm demander." Judith Kleinfeld first coined this term in 1975 while working with indigenous students in Alaska. Kleinfeld (1975) found that the teachers who were most successful had strong relationships with their students while also having expectations of them.

In the last few years, as educators have taken a more whole-child approach to education, the idea of being a warm demander has seen a resurgence. The concept has even been expanded to include educational leaders as warm demanders as well (Safir, 2019).

Sadly, not all days are going to go as well as you would like. So, what about days that are full of disruptive or defiant behavior? What about the days when you struggle to engage your students and you're totally off your A game? Tomorrow is another day. It's important for all students to know that tomorrow is a new day and a fresh start for both you and them. This consistency will pay off – especially with students affected by trauma or poverty. As you get to know your students, you will begin to learn the subtle nuances and changes in behavior that may indicate your student is about to engage in disruptive, avoidant, or defiant behavior. Once you learn these signs, you will learn how to manage and support students before they reach their (and possibly your) breaking point.

Conclusion

The importance of relationships cannot be denied. The positive effects of relationships in the classroom and with students have been well researched. Students do better academically and are less likely to engage in high-risk behaviors when they feel connected to school through positive relationships. As educators, it is our responsibility to establish and maintain boundaries with our students. It protects us professionally and personally. Several guidelines were shared on how to establish boundaries. It's important to be aware of behaviors or even words that push your buttons so that you can find proactive strategies to handle them.

There are a multitude of strategies you can use to get to know your students. Establishing rapport, providing an opportunity for students to share their expectations, using a strengths-based perspective, and being a warm demander will help create a culture and climate in your classroom that can lead to better student outcomes. These strategies can be done at any time of the year and many can be employed more than once. After all, our students are changing and growing every day.

Self-Reflection

1. What boundaries do you have? How can you maintain them while still connecting with students?
2. What strategies might you use to build relationships and connections with your students?
3. Think of a student with whom you struggle. What are their hidden strengths?
4. In what ways are you a warm demander?

References

Battistich, V., Schaps, E., & Wilson, N. (2004). Effects of an elementary school intervention on students' "connectedness" to school and social adjustment during middle school. *The Journal of Primary Prevention, 24*(3), 243–262.

Birch, S.H. & Ladd, G.W. (1997). The teacher–child relationship and early school adjustment. *Journal of School Psychology, 55*(1), 61–79.

Blum, R. (2005). *School connectedness: Improving the lives of students.* Baltimore, MD: Johns Hopkins Bloomberg School of Public Health.

Child Welfare Gateway (2015, April). *Understanding the effects of maltreatment on brain development.* Retrieved April 29, 2019, from www. childwelfare.gov/pubPDFs/brain_development.pdf

Curby, T.W., Rimm-Kaufman, S.E., & Ponitz, C.C. (2009). Teacher–child interactions and children's achievement trajectories across kindergarten and first grade. *Journal of Educational Psychology, 101*(4), 912–925.

Donohue, K.M., Perry, K.E., & Weinstein, R.S. (2003). Teachers' classroom practices and children's rejection by their peers. *Applied Developmental Psychology, 24,* 91–118.

Ewing, A.R. & Taylor, A.R. (2009). The role of child gender and ethnicity in teacher–child relationship quality and children's behavioral adjustment in preschool. *Early Childhood Research Quarterly, 24*(1), 92–105.

Frisby, B.N. & Martin, M.M. (2010). Instructor–student and student–student rapport in the classroom. *Communication Education, 59*(2), 146–164. doi: 10.1080/03634520903564362

Gregory, A., Allen, J.P., Mikami, A.Y., Hafen, C.A., & Pianta, R.C. (2013). Effects of a professional development program on behavioral engagement of students in middle and high school. *Psychology in the Schools, 51*(2), 143–163. doi: 10.1002/pits.21741

Hammond, W. & Zimmerman, R. (n.d.) *A strengths-based perspective.* Retrieved February 1, 2020, from www.esd.ca/Programs/Resiliency/ Documents/RSL_STRENGTH_BASED_PERSPECTIVE.pdf

Hamre, B.K. & Pianta, R.C. (2001). Early teacher-child relationships and the trajectory of children's school outcomes through eighth grade. *Child Development, 72,* 625–638.

Hamre, B.K. & Pianta, R.C. (2006). Student-teacher relationships. In G.G. Bear & K.M. Minke (Eds.), *Children's needs III: Development, prevention, and intervention* (pp. 59–71). Bethesda, MD: National Association of School Psychologists.

Hughes, J.N., Cavell, T.A., & Wilson, V. (2001). Further support for the developmental significance of the quality of the teacher–student relationship. *Journal of School Psychology*, *39*(4), 289–301.

Khan-Baker, A. (2016, August 12). *Why pronouncing students' names is important to building relationships*. Retrieved January 25, 2020, from www.nbpts.org/why-pronouncing-students-names-is-important-to-building-relationships/

Kleinfeld, J. (1975). Effective teachers of Eskimo and Indian students. *School Review*, *83*(2), 301–344. Retrieved January 10, 2020, from www.jstor.org/stable/1084645?read-now=1&seq=1#page_scan_tab_contents

McLaughlin, C. (2017). *The lasting impact of mispronouncing students' names*. Retrieved February 1, 2020, from http://neatoday.org./2016/09/01/pronouncing-students-names/

Nadler, R.S. (2011). *Leading with emotional intelligence: Hands-on strategies for building confident and collaborative star performers*. New York: McGraw-Hill.

Nowak, C. (2017, April 3). *Here's why you NEED to drink water when you're stressed*. Retrieved March 30, 2020, from www.thehealthy.com/mental-health/stress/drink-water-reduce-stress/

Rudasill, K.M., Reio, T.G., Stipanovic, N., & Taylor, J.E. (2010). A longitudinal study of student-teacher relationship quality, difficult temperament, and risky behavior from childhood to early adolescence. *Journal of School Psychology*, *48*(5), 389–412.

Safir, S. (2019, March). Becoming a warm demander. *Educational Leadership*, *76*(6), 64–69.

2

How Do You Do It? Building Connections *between* Students

It's not enough that you, as an adult in the building, have a strong relationship with your students. You also want your students to have good relations with their fellow classmates. This chapter will introduce some quick strategies to build connections between peers. Bonus! Remember how in Chapter 1 we discussed how positive relationships can literally rewire neural connections? Well, positive peer relationships can have the same effect!

Peer relatedness is stronger in classrooms where helping behaviors are valued, and where students have opportunities to interact academically with one another. There are easy-to-implement strategies you can use in your classroom that foster relationships between students and teachers, and among peers, and that create a climate of relatedness. A few of the activities to build relationships in this chapter can also create relatedness. The sharing of biopoems could connect students by providing them with information that they may not have known about their peers.

Hey, Me Too!

"Hey, Me Too!" is a strategy that can help students see what they may have in common with others. This strategy also establishes rapport. It helps students see that, oftentimes, they are more like their peers than they first realized. By allowing students to design their own double-sided emojis and attach them to a popsicle stick, they can quickly create a fun tool that they can use to show agreement or disagreement with a given statement. Agreement/ disagreement can be shown several ways. Students may choose to use basic (appropriate) emojis they are familiar with on their smartphones or devices. The response tool could also have an image of something they like on one side and dislike on the other. The only criterion is that students would need to explain what their images indicate. For example, a bright sunshiny beach on one side might indicate agreement, while a snowman might show disagreement because they do not like cold weather. Older students may be motivated to use a favorite sports team or band to show agreement on one side, and a rival team or band they do not care for to show disagreement ("Go UK Wildcats!"). See Figure 2.1 for an example of simple agreement and disagreement emojis.

Once the emoji response tools have been created, they can be used for academic and non-academic questions. Students can respond individually, giving you a quick formative assessment. Some low-risk questions may be:

◆ Does pineapple belong on pizza? (There may be some strong opinions on this one!)
◆ Morning is the best time of the day.
◆ There should be more time between classes.
◆ We should have a week-long Fall Break every year.
◆ I think summer is the best time of year.
◆ I would like to be famous one day.

Academic concepts can be used to gather information on where students are in their learning. This also creates connectedness because it is a non-threatening way to share your thinking and

FIGURE 2.1
Examples of Agreement and Disagreement Emojis

to visualize that you are most likely not alone in your thoughts. Some examples of academic content could be:

◆ I like turning in assignments online instead of in written form.
◆ I need more practice with today's math skill.
◆ I would have liked living in the early 1800s.
◆ If I could've chosen, I would have lived in the Northwest Pacific Coast Native American region.
◆ I would like to work with a partner during tomorrow's class.
◆ I would like the option of working with different manipulatives.
◆ I would have survived the Oregon Trail.

Once students become comfortable with responding individually, the teacher can then encourage them to share out verbally the reasons for their agreement or disagreement. The idea is that, once they begin seeing the commonalities in their thoughts and beliefs with their peers, they will be more likely to share their thinking because they have a sense of relatedness they may not have experienced before. This type of formative assessment can also provide the teacher with an idea on how to group students for different projects or assignments, based on their individual responses.

This strategy is very helpful for students affected by trauma or poverty, or who receive special education services. It provides a non-threatening way to share their ideas and feelings. They may also feel a sense of competency as they are able to participate with their same-age peers.

Hey, Me Too! is a very low-tech strategy to engage students in sharing their thinking and making connections with their peers, and even their teacher. There are many digital tools available for eliciting the same type of responses. Those will be introduced in Chapter 5 in connection with putting it all together and scaffolding collaboration strategies.

Would You Rather?

Another low-tech/low-prep activity that fosters relatedness is a game called "Would You Rather?" The premise is to give students two options to decide between, and for them to rationalize their reason behind their choice. This game is directly connected to metacognition, because we are getting students to think about their thinking and supporting them in being able to articulate why they made their particular choice. Because of the lack of human interaction and discourse many of our students experience in their home environments, they most likely aren't given choices, nor are they ever asked to share their reasoning for a decision. Being able to make choices and share their reasoning helps build new neural pathways in the brain, and can make existing neural pathways more efficient.

Would You Rather? questions engage all students, are low risk, and are simply fun for our students. Some example questions to start with could be:

♦ Would you rather be able to eat only pizza or ice cream?
♦ Would you rather be invisible or be able to fly?

◆ Would you rather be hot or cold all the time?
◆ Would you rather eat everything with a spoon or drink it in a cup?

This is also a great way to incorporate movement during the school day in a time-efficient manner. For example,

> Would you rather eat spaghetti with a straw, or use a fork to eat soup? If you would rather use a fork to eat soup, please stand up. If you would rather eat spaghetti with a straw, please line up for lunch.

You can keep students on their toes by mixing up the directions you give to each group. This builds in a sense of novelty. Novelty helps students get engaged in class content (Kaye, 2018).

Once students have become familiar with the procedure, you can start bringing in academic content. Some examples may include:

◆ Would you rather live in the Southwest Native American geographical region or Eastern Woodland region?
◆ Would you rather measure a football field with a ruler or measure a paperclip with a yardstick?
◆ Would you rather be an antagonist or a protagonist in a story?
◆ Would you rather be a liquid or a solid?

Again, this is an easy-to-implement activity that is inclusive of all students. Over time, students will become more confident with sharing the reasoning behind their choices. Hopefully, teachers may begin to see students generalizing their reasoning skills in other content areas or aspects of their daily lives.

Special Interests or Hobbies

Determining students' special interests or hobbies is another way to foster relatedness among our students. Simple "getting-to-know-you" activities provide students the opportunity to share what makes them unique or to connect them with a peer who has a similar interest. Identifying and acknowledging what motivates or inspires our youth is a critical step in building relationships. By asking questions or sharing information, we are letting them know that we care. We are also validating who they are as a human being, that they are worthy of our time, and that they matter.

Student interests may also create a picture or bring to light an understanding of someone's behavior and/or belief system. A student's restlessness and constant tapping of objects on a desk may appear to be a nervous habit or a mere intentional annoyance. Once we start unveiling student interests, we might realize this student has been taking drum lessons from a very early age. To capitalize on this understanding (and hidden strength) would include planning more tactile experiences and activities for this student and others who might benefit from differentiated instruction. Another example may be finding out that a student does not have access to the internet at home. You quickly understand her interest in always choosing computer or tablet activities at workstations, and the reason for the behavior meltdown that ensues when she is redirected to another activity, or restricted from an internet-based activity that would best be completed in another mode.

Tools 2.2 and 2.3 show examples of some special interests and hobbies cards that could be used with students as conversation starters.

Classroom Bingo

Many back-to-school/getting-to-know-you activities include classroom bingo. In this version of bingo, you must search for someone in the room who meets specified criteria. Some examples might be finding someone who has sisters; someone who likes playing kickball; someone who doesn't like ice cream; or someone who did not attend an elementary school in your district. With one glance or review of the information that students gather from this activity, educators can easily start fostering connectedness among peers within the class and possibly different classes by providing opportunities for students to share a common interest or belief. We've included an example of a classroom bingo sheet in Tool 2.4.

Tool 2.2 Special Interest and Hobbies Questions for Younger Students

Questions for younger students

What is your favorite flavor of ice cream?	Which do you like better, Science or Social Studies?	What month is your birthday?	Doritos or Fritos?
What is your favorite movie?	How many brothers and sisters do you have?	Hot dog or hamburger?	What is your favorite thing to do during outside recess?
What is your favorite candy?	What time is your bedtime?	Cats or dogs?	Who is your favorite cartoon character?
If you could be one animal, what would it be?	What is your favorite book?	What do you do after school?	What sport do you play or would like to play?

Class Calendar

Having a shared class calendar can also foster a sense of related-ness in your classroom. You can determine what you would like to include on the calendar. You can include birthdays, activities that your students are involved in, such as sporting events, music or dance recitals, and important community events.

Tool 2.3   Examples of Special Interest and Hobbies Questions for Older Students

Questions for older students

What is your favorite (appropriate) saying?	What is your favorite day of the week?	What is one course you wish you were not required to take?	What is one course you wish was offered?
Is there a celebrity you follow on social media? Who?	If you had the option to choose a new name what would it be?	What food do you wish was served every day of the week?	Is a hot dog a sandwich?
Whose shoes would you want to walk in for a day?	Netflix or movie theater?	What sport or activity do you wish was offered?	What invention would make your life easier?
What is essential to have in your locker or backpack?	If you were a teacher, what is one thing you would be sure to tell your students?	Do you plan to register and start voting when you turn 18? Why or why not?	Who do you admire and why?

Tool 2.4   Classroom Bingo

Find someone in our class who…

is the oldest child	wears glasses or contacts	likes scary movies	likes to sing	eats sushi
has an after-school job	can whistle	is left-handed	was born in another state	likes to cook
is an only child	likes black jelly beans	free space	has a pet that is not a cat or dog	was born in the same month as you
has been on a plane	likes to read	has Math as their favorite subject	plays a sport	plays a musical instrument
has green eyes	can do a magic trick	walks to school	likes to read	is the youngest child

Student Partnerships

Some other time-efficient strategies to promote connectedness include providing opportunities for peer tutoring and using a variety of methods for creating partnerships based on interests and beliefs, and not necessarily on academic ability. Students could also be assigned "buddies" for when one of them is absent to help them catch up by sharing assignments, updates on projects, or notes missed.

Seating Arrangements

Another strategy might be to mix up the seating arrangement to encourage new connections for each unit of learning. Working with others, especially those different from us, is a lifelong skill that students need opportunities to practice in the school setting because, depending on their home environment and support system, they may have limited opportunities to network with others or none at all.

Conclusion

The relationships among the students in your classroom are as equally important as your relationship to your students. Peer relatedness is an important factor in creating a safe and supportive classroom environment. It's also necessary for student engagement. Several low-cost and easy-to-implement strategies were shared. These strategies take into account similarities between students and help students make connections with one another. In the next chapter we will discuss strategies to help get your classroom ready for collaborative learning.

Self-Reflection

1. What are some strategies that you already use to foster a sense of peer relatedness in your classroom?
2. Which of the strategies in this chapter might you implement in your classroom?
3. How might you know that you have made connections among the students in your classroom?

Reference

Kaye, C. (2018, March 2). *Surprise! How novelty can help students learn.* Retrieved December 19, 2019, from www.eschoolnews.com/2018/03/05/surprise-novelty-can-help-students-learn/

3

Laying the Foundation for Collaborative Learning

Students cannot be expected to walk into a classroom for the first time and successfully participate in a collaborative group or even with a partner. Many adults have deficits with this skill as well. No matter the age of the child, many factors, as mentioned before, determine their capacity to work in a group. Many of our students do not experience structure at home and may not have even in their previous years of learning. Structure is what many of our students with behavior or emotional issues or disabilities crave and deserve. Establishing classroom expectations is a necessity from the very beginning, and student input must be sought out and valued. In Chapter 2, we discussed the idea of getting student input as it relates to student involvement in their learning. In this chapter, the process will be slightly different, as we discuss getting student insight on how all of the students should be expected to behave while in class.

Norms

What are norms? Most of us have a set of rules or structures that guide our behavior in various environments, whether at home or in different social settings. For example, norms dictate how you behave at church, or how you act when you're with your friends at a concert. While there may be some similarities in expected behavior (for example, you may sing at both places), mostly, expected behavior is different. The Merriam-Webster online dictionary (n.d.) defines a norm as:

1: *an authoritative standard: MODEL*
2: *a principle of right action binding upon the members of a group and serving to guide, control, or regulate proper and acceptable behavior*
3: *AVERAGE: such as*
    a: *a set standard of development or achievement usually derived from the average or median achievement of a large group*
    b: *a pattern or trait taken to be typical in the behavior of a social group*
    c: *a widespread or usual practice, procedure, or custom*

Schools largely operate under middle-class norms, which Ruby Payne (2013) refers to as hidden rules. Not all of our students understand what these hidden rules are. Hidden rules are unspoken clues that are understood and demonstrated by members of a group. Think about the student coming from a family of generational poverty who comes to school with an Apple Watch, but who has not paid for a field trip the entire school year. This example demonstrates the value people living in generational poverty have for possessions and things. People coming from a middle-class background tend to value work and achievement.

Anyone who has been to the city shopping mall, local grocery store, or even sporting events has probably observed that not everyone holds the same models of acceptable behavior. There may be an apparent average or pattern of typical behavior; however, based on your social class, the norm for any given situation may be understood (or misunderstood). Most of us have probably given the side-eye to the family of six eating at Golden Corral in celebration of the middle child's birthday, with their many trips to the buffet for the kids, uneaten food on the table, and conversations about family business that can be heard tables away.

Educators witness the same discrepancy in hidden rules and norms in their classrooms every day. Even the type of register (language that we use) varies depending on social class and social situations. Unless the differences are addressed, students will not be aware of their own hidden rules and the middle-class norms that are expected at school and work. An additional hidden rule held by families living in poverty is the value placed on relationships; hence the reason why fifth-grader Javon really didn't want his teacher calling Mamaw to report any misbehaviors. Educators can benefit from understanding the hidden rules of social classes, to build classroom relationships and a set of agreed-upon and understood norms to create a classroom environment of learning (Payne, 2013).

Strategies for Determining Classroom Norms

Research indicates the following:

- ◆ Teachers who establish and maintain norms for an effective learning environment spend more time teaching, because less time is usurped by discipline (Brophy, 2000).
- ◆ Norms that engender a supportive learning environment include acting and interacting responsibly, treating others with respect and concern, and fostering a learning orientation (Brophy, 1998, 2000; Good & Brophy, 2000; Sergiovanni, 1994).

Keeping these in mind, teachers must be clear about the purpose of establishing norms and determine negotiables and non-negotiables when generating student input. It might be a non-negotiable that they will have a quiz every week. It might be negotiable that the class may choose to listen to school-appropriate music while working on projects. One strategy to create buy-in with students is for them to write on an index card what they need from their teacher in order to learn. On another index card, they can describe what type of interactions in the classroom will be conducive to learning. At the same time, the teacher records on chart paper what they need from students, individually and as a whole class. Students can then take their index cards and tape them to corresponding items. This creates transparency with both teacher and student expectations. This strategy can also be used by tech-savvy teachers through Google Docs, Google Forms, or an add-on such as Pear Deck. Students can respond anonymously, and still communicate their needs.

Once classroom norms and expectations have been established and explicitly communicated to all stakeholders, including parents, students then decide their commitment to upholding the agreed-upon norms. On a Consensogram, students can determine their level of commitment on a scale of 1 to 4. An example of the Consensogram can be found in Figure 3.1.

Of course we would want students to commit to a 3 or 4, but we also need to be realistic, and students need to know we understand that sometimes a Wednesday may feel like a dreaded Monday, or what happened in the previous class may carry over to another learning environment. This activity is also a good way to determine if norms need to be tweaked or revisited. If a majority of students are consistently rating themselves as 1 or 2 on the Consensogram, revisiting the norms may be necessary. It could be that the norms were too restrictive or maybe even a little too ambiguous. Another option for low adherence to norms could be that the adults are inconsistent in enforcing them.

For students experiencing social-emotional issues or difficulty regulating behavior, this commitment can be very powerful in building relationships. They can indicate what level of commitment they have each day, and if it is below 3, then a

Commitment to Classroom Norms and Expectations

1	2	3	4
Least effort	Depends on the day	I'll try my best	Most effort

FIGURE 3.1
Consensogram for Norms

plan can be developed that acknowledges where they are in their head space, but still communicates what their expectations are for the day. It's not a free pass to disregard the norms and disrupt the learning environment.

Establishing norms is beneficial for students affected by trauma. If we want these students to be successful in our classrooms, we need to ensure that they feel safe, competent, and worthy. Norms provide a sense of safety, which in turn provides consistency and predictability, allowing students to focus on content. Norms also provide an opportunity for students who may have behavior challenges or a history of trauma to experience competence, as they provide a clear framework for expected behaviors.

Grade Level Examples of Norms

"I have classroom rules posted. Aren't these the norms or what is expected behavior in the classroom?" No. Rules are often posted as behaviors that aren't acceptable. Norms are behaviors that one would expect to see in a productive learning environment and are generally stated in the positive.

Norms in a kindergarten class may include:
We will follow directions.
We will take turns during activities.
We will use kind words.
We will work together.

Of course, for each of these, specific examples and non-examples would be needed to demonstrate what is expected in a variety of situations. Visual examples are also an asset for younger students or students with special needs who may need a reminder of what the expectations look like.

Norms in intermediate or secondary classrooms will consist of many of the same elements in order to create a productive learning environment; however, the language needs to be specific and relevant to the age group.

Norms in a ninth-grade Math classroom:
We will be respectful with our words and actions.
We will learn from our mistakes.
We will be on time with necessary materials.
We will work together.

With older students, gathering their input is critical. Many of our students have very strong opinions and teachers must be flexible and responsive in eliciting feedback from them, as well as having students help define what the norms look and sound like. What students deem as respectful might vary from student to student and might not be aligned with the teacher's perception either. Establishing common expectations and being consistent in our actions is the best way to ensure our classroom expectations foster a culture of learning shared by all stakeholders in the classroom.

Class Meetings

"I don't have time in the day for a class meeting." With the urgency educators feel to teach content, many may think there isn't time to spend on "non-instructional" tasks. How beneficial would it be to reserve a specific time to address academic and social topics? Here are just a few benefits of a class meeting:

◆ Gives students a voice in classroom decision making.
◆ Builds confidence and self-esteem within students.
◆ Creates transparency and trust with all stakeholders.
◆ Cultivates speaking and listening skills.
◆ Creates a structure for addressing issues that may impede learning.
◆ Fosters leadership skills.
◆ Provides an opportunity to practice social-emotional learning.
◆ Increases instructional time.

Possible Sentence Starters for Elementary Class Meetings

"A problem on the playground is _____."
"I agree with _____ because _____."
"A different idea we could use is _____."
"I disagree with _____ because_____."

FIGURE 3.2
Sentence Stems for Elementary Class Meetings

Class meetings can be a great equalizer for students and are a good way to ensure equity and inclusion (Durden, 2017). They provide an opportunity for all students, regardless of ability level or special education status, to provide input. Class meetings are a great way to help build trust and create a sense of community (Edwards & Mullis, 2003). As an educator, you can gain insight into what students consider to be problems and the dynamics between students. There are a variety of things you can do in a class meeting. Plan, make decisions, solve problems, and share information are all possibilities. They can be a regularly scheduled part of the day, or they can be something that is done on an as-needed basis. Some schools, such as those that are implementing the Olweus Bullying Prevention Program, build class-meeting time into their master schedules.

Class meetings will look different depending on the age of students. Younger students may need sentence starters. See Figure 3.2 for some ideas.

Sentence starters, or talking prompts, could also be used to scaffold older students in leading the conversations. The teacher is the facilitator allowing opportunities for leadership skills, the practice of listening and speaking skills, and empowering students to have a voice in their learning environment.

Considerations for Implementing Class Meetings

Time of meeting: What time of day is best for you to hold your class meetings? Some teachers prefer to start their day or class period with a class meeting, while some prefer to end their day or class period with a class meeting. After lunch and after recess are also good times to hold class meetings; they give students a chance to refocus before engaging in more academically engaging tasks. The good thing is, if you try a time and it doesn't work out, you can experiment with different times throughout the day to find the right fit for your class or class period.

Length of meeting: You'll want your meeting to be long enough that the topic is covered, but short enough that students don't lose interest and become disengaged. The time of day and day of week that you hold your class meetings may have an impact on how long you and your students can realistically meet.

Seating arrangement: The traditional seating arrangement is for all students and teachers to sit together in a large circle. This can be achieved either by sitting on the floor or by putting the desks into a circle. It is vital to the class-meeting process that all of the participants in your class meeting sit in a circle. The act of sitting in a circle helps with equality and responsibility, and also helps the teacher take on more of a facilitator role (Costello, Wachtel, & Wachtel, 2019). For students who have been affected by trauma, the act of sitting in a circle may provide a sense of safety as they will be able to see all of the participants quickly.

Norms: Just as you have classroom norms, you will work with your class on developing norms for participating in the class meeting. You would want to develop these at the first class meeting you have. It doesn't have to be a formal process; it is something that can be done quickly. These guidelines for behavior should be brought out and quickly reviewed at the start of each class meeting. Having them in writing on chart paper will help participants refer back to them if others start to violate them. You will also want your class to consider what each of the selected norms looks like. For example, if one of the norms is that only one person can talk at a time, how will that be enforced? Will you use some type of object for students to hold when it's their turn to talk (such as a stuffed animal, talking chips, or a talking stick)? The norms may include things like:

- Just one person should speak at a time.
- What happens in the circle, stays in the circle.
- Don't be disrespectful.

Structure: Consideration will want to be given to how your class meeting is structured. How will students know when it's time to get in the circle? Will you have a greeting or class affirmation to start the meeting? How will students know when the class-meeting time is over?

Topics: It will be helpful as you start your class meetings to have predetermined topics for the first few meetings. If you choose to start the class meetings at the beginning of the school year, class expectations, peer relatedness discussions, and school information would all be acceptable topics. Student-generated concerns and issues are also encouraged, especially as the year progresses and students become more comfortable with you, their classmates, and the class-meeting process. You will want to discuss with students how they might be able to submit ideas for future discussions, such as a suggestion box, which was discussed in Chapter 1. Additional resources for class-meeting topics can be found in Appendix B. We've also included a class-meeting planning tool in Tool 3.3.

There will be some skills that your students may need additional practice in to get the most out of the class-meeting process. These will be addressed in Chapter 4. They include active listening, empathy, and paraphrasing.

Conclusion

There are several strategies that are essential to laying the foundation for effective collaborative learning. Setting and communicating classroom expectations, by establishing norms with all classroom stakeholders, is just the beginning. Developing an understanding of our culturally diverse populations can aid you in looking beyond the bodies that walk through the

Tool 3.3   Class-Meeting Planning Tool

Class/Morning Meeting Plan

Date:

Period/Class:

Topic:

Related Content Standard:

Resources Needed:

Agenda Item	Person Responsible
Greeting	
Review of Meeting Norms/Rules	
Introduction of Topic	
Review of Decisions Made	
Follow-Up Needed:	
Closing	

Reflection:

Did all students have an opportunity to participate and voice concerns? If not, what might be done differently to ensure 100% participation?

Were students able to follow the meeting norms/rules?

Did other topics for future meetings come up during the meeting?

door, and seeing what experiences, beliefs, and baggage that enter as well. In the next chapter we will focus on the skills that students need to be successful, not only in your classroom, but also in life.

Self-Reflection

1. How have you gotten student input for classroom norms? If you haven't, how might you do that in the future?
2. What might be some additional benefits for having students assist with developing norms and holding class meetings?
3. What topics would you like to cover during a class meeting?

References

Brophy, J.E. (1998). *Motivating students to learn*. Boston, MA: McGraw-Hill.

Brophy, J.E. (2000). *Teaching*. Geneva, Switzerland: International Bureau of Education.

Costello, B., Wachtel, J., & Wachtel, T. (2019). *Restorative circles in schools: Building community and enhancing learning*. Bethlehem, PA: International Institute for Restorative Practices.

Durden, F. (2017). *Morning meetings for special education classrooms: 101 fun ideas, creative activities and adaptable techniques*. Berkeley, CA: Ulysses Press.

Edwards, D. & Mullis, F. (2003). Classroom meetings: Encouraging a climate of cooperation. *Professional School Counseling, 7*(1), 20–28.

Good, T.L. & Brophy, J.E. (2000). *Looking in classrooms* (8th ed.). New York: Longman.

Norm. (n.d.). In *Merriam-Webster.com dictionary*. Retrieved April 25, 2019, from www.merriam-webster.com/dictionary/norms?src=search-dict-box

Payne, R.K. (2013). *Framework for understanding poverty*. Highlands, TX: aha! Process.

Sergiovanni, T. (1994). *Building community in schools*. San Francisco, CA: Jossey-Bass.

4

Making Sure Your Students Have the Necessary Essential Skills

How much easier would our teaching and helping careers be if we could walk into our classrooms on the first day of school to find all of our students, regardless of background, having the necessary essential skills to function in a collaborative setting? Wouldn't it be great if we could just dive right into content? Unfortunately, we know it just doesn't work that way. You can't put students into collaborative-learning groups and expect them to know how to behave or engage in academic learning. You will have students in your class who lack the interpersonal skills needed for group work. There could be a variety of different reasons for this. For example, trauma-affected students may be withdrawn and lack the ability to trust their peers. Students affected by poverty may lack the language skills necessary to communicate. Students receiving special education services may lack interpersonal or communication skills. Making sure your students have these essential skills is a great way to incorporate social-emotional learning (SEL). Oftentimes, SEL is seen as an add-on or something extra that needs to be taught. In reality, SEL is something that can and should be embedded in every content area and throughout the school day. For additional resources on SEL, see Appendix B.

Some skills that students will need are:

◆ Active listening – listening to understand.
◆ How to disagree politely.
◆ How to engage in productive academic conversations.
◆ How to be a good team member.
◆ Perspective taking.
◆ Empathy.

Active Listening and Academic Conversations

Before we begin demonstrating how students should speak to each other, the first skill they need to be trained on is listening. Students need to know how to listen to understand, not to listen to merely hear the words someone is using. Thomas Gordon (2016) coined the term "active listening" and describes it as "reflecting back the meaning and feeling of group members in order to test out the leader's understanding of their messages." In our current digital world, how often do we, as adults, believe we can effectively multitask? How many times has a wife detailed the kids' weekly schedule to a husband who's watching television, only to find, days later, that he has no recall of the baseball game the following night or of the kids' weekly schedule? How often do we see parents checking email or social media on their smartphones while their child is fussing about an event that happened in the girls' restroom earlier in the day? Current technology and the business of daily life has stripped us of listening skills.

Effective listening skills are key to building relationships between any individuals. By suspending activities, the listener is showing interest, concern, and curiosity. Many of our students haven't had effective listening skills modeled for them and this could be a barrier in the relationships they build with adults and peers. Most state academic standards include speaking and listening skills progressing throughout every grade level. The premise of these standards is most likely to prepare students for real-world collaborations and the ability to acquire effective communication skills. One piece of being an effective communicator must include listening skills. What are good listening skills? How do students acquire them? Simply, they must be explicitly taught and reinforced as they progress through their academic careers. Below are some suggested listening skills that could be taught across grade levels and content areas.

1. Ignore distractions (other people, interruptions, technology).
2. Maintain eye contact.
3. Focus to understand to be able to paraphrase or summarize.
4. Pay attention to words that might indicate emotion.
5. Pay attention to body language.

What deficits do your students have in listening skills? How would instruction of these skills look in an elementary setting as opposed to a secondary setting?

Regardless of the grade level you work with, application of these steps requires numerous opportunities of modeling and practice. Educators must think about what each of these steps might look like, or how to communicate them depending on the age of their students. No matter their age, students need to realize all the benefits of being a good listener. Not only do listening skills help us learn better, these skills also improve our attention span by blocking out distractions and biases that we may hold.

Steps in quality listening require providing feedback in the forms of asking clarifying questions and validating ideas and feelings. Many of our students, whether they are living in poverty, have been affected by trauma, or have a learning disability or language barrier, may not have acquired the vocabulary or language skills to communicate effectively – hence reinforcing the imperative for us to teach our students how to talk to each other. How is this done?

One easy strategy is modeling and being explicit with the vocabulary you use. Students will rise to rigorous vocabulary usage if it is modeled, practiced, and expected. Beyond modeling, providing students with a toolbox of sentence stems in order to aid them in practicing in real-life contexts is helpful. Sentence stems could be created for general discussions and practiced in the class meetings as discussed in Chapter 3. Some examples include: "I agree with _____ because _____" or "I disagree because _____."

Content-specific sentence stems can also be used to promote academic vocabulary. A few examples might include: "The antagonist in the story struggled with _____"; "The hypothesis was flawed because _____"; "The misconception in this worked math problem might be _____"; "Cultural conflict occurred during this time period between_____ ____ and _____ because _____."

All students would benefit from having the stems posted on a chart as a visible reminder of the expectation of use. It might also be a good idea to make them available on index cards for use in small-group work. With repeated and practiced use of these language tools, students are not only being supported in their language skills, but also with transferring that spoken language into their writing. Tool 4.1 provides some content-specific sentence stems. Figure 4.2 offers an example of how they could look in the classroom.

Another skill that would be beneficial to share with older students is the art of paraphrasing. Paraphrasing is not restating someone's ideas, thoughts, or words verbatim. Paraphrasing is communicating, meaning using your own words. This is a skill that we need to begin teaching students as soon as possible to deter from the practice of plagiarism, or an accidental act of plagiarism. Students of all ages can practice paraphrasing verbally. One activity that could be built into any content area is "Turn and Talk" to a partner. Identify partners as A and B. Partner A is the responder and Partner B is the listener. Partner B uses active listening skills and then paraphrases Partner A's response. Partner A then confirms if the paraphrase was accurate. Partners then switch roles, providing the opportunity to practice communicating a thought, active listening, and paraphrasing.

Explicitly teaching students how to listen and how to talk to each other supports relationship building in the classroom, promotes improved learning, and fosters team building.

Tool 4.1 Content-Specific Sentence Starter

Literacy	Mathematics
➢ What evidence in the text supports your idea? ➢ Is there another perspective you may consider? ➢ What do you believe was the author's intention with _____?	➢ Explain why you chose this strategy and how do you know it worked? ➢ What information in the problem helped you decide how to start? ➢ Is there another way you could have come up with this solution?
Science	Social Studies
➢ How did you decide the steps for your scientific method? ➢ What key words helped you identify _____? ➢ Can you provide evidence to prove this is the best solution?	➢ What key words in the primary source helped you come to this conclusion? ➢ Can you identify cultural influences that impacted this event? What are they? ➢ Who might have a different perspective during this time period?

Another related benefit that could result is improved classroom behavior. When students feel cared for and valued, and are able to use appropriate words while engaging in conversations with adults and peers, a classroom culture of learning has been created.

How to Disagree Politely

Another skill that is essential both in the classroom and in life is knowing how to disagree politely without being offensive. This skill can be tricky for some of us to teach as we weren't

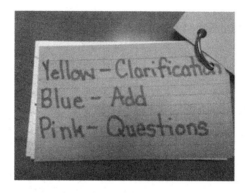

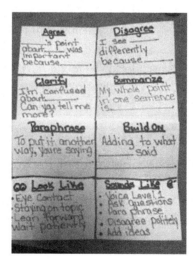

FIGURE 4.2
Class Examples of Sentence Stems

taught this explicitly. Technology can further complicate this skill for many of us. Kid President has a great video to help students understand this concept. It can be found on YouTube. The idea of disagreeing politely is also covered in many social-emotional curriculums. The best way to teach your students how to disagree politely is to provide copious amounts of opportunity to practice disagreeing in a safe, supportive environment. Engaging in both scripted and unscripted role playing is a wonderful method for practicing. Starting first with scripted role play will provide a scaffolded support for students who have communication or processing delays. Teaching our students how to disagree using the sentence stems from the section on academic conversations may prove beneficial. When you first start teaching students how to engage in this skill, you will want to begin with non-academic content. You want your students to focus on the process and skills needed to disagree with someone without being offensive, and not whether they have the right answer to a content-based question. For example, role playing a discussion on which ice cream flavor you prefer, or which baseball team is your favorite, would be helpful. Another option is to use optical-illusion pictures that we see floating around the internet. Was the dress blue or gold? Do you see an elderly woman or a young woman? As students become more familiar and get comfortable with disagreeing, you can move to more academic content.

How to be a Productive Team Member

Many of our students come into our classrooms with no idea of how to be a team player. We all have experiences with students who have no idea how to accept responsibility for their behavior, how to make decisions, how to communicate effectively, or how to divide the workload in a fair manner. One of the easiest ways to achieve this is to assign each student a role during group work. This is effective for students of any age. Some roles you may want to have are timekeeper, recorder, speaker, and a materials manager. This provides a manner in which all students are held responsible and accountable for the work to be completed. Before setting students free to do their group work, have a discussion on what the duties are of each role. Be sure to elicit feedback and input on what the responsibilities of each role are. During group work, be sure to look for hidden strengths. You may be surprised at what skills and talents your students possess. Chapter 6 will describe some specific activities where role assignments may be helpful.

Perspective Taking

All of the concepts we've already discussed in this chapter will aid in teaching perspective taking. In Chapter 2, we discussed several strategies that provide the opportunity for perspective taking. The "Would You Rather?" strategy is one that is really powerful in teaching this concept. Even the Would You Rather? questions of a non-academic nature are beneficial in providing practice and giving students a sense of competence. As students get more comfortable with expressing their perspectives, they will be ready to move onto more academic-based perspective taking. Eventually, students should be able to compare and contrast different literary or historical characters. Being empathetic will aid them in this skill. We will discuss that essential skill next.

Empathy

Empathy, or the ability to understand what someone else is feeling, is one of the most important essential skills that we can instill in our students. Perspective taking is a large component of having empathy (Ditkowsky, 2018). Another effective way to teach empathy is to have your students engage in a service-learning project. One of the great benefits is that students of any age, skill level, or life circumstance can participate. The service-learning project provides a chance for students to practice every essential skill discussed in this chapter. There are numerous

options for projects and numerous ways for students to participate. Some possible options include hosting a donation drive for
a local food bank, animal shelter, homeless shelter, or children's
hospital. Students may choose to organize and participate in an
awareness walk. They may also want to volunteer in a nursing
home, animal shelter, or at the local library.

The possibilities are seemingly endless and can be a little
overwhelming. The first step in deciding which service-learning
project to engage in would be getting your students to conduct
some community research. You may want them to create a poll
to see what the needs are in your community. If that seems too
overwhelming, creating a survey that just teachers or their families respond to might help. Students might conduct interviews
with specific people in your school, such as the family resource
coordinator or the school social worker.

Once students have some ideas of what the community
needs, it's time to engage in brainstorming. Ask students to
develop a list of all the ideas that they have to meet the identified
needs. Once you have a list of possible projects, get students to
vote on their favorite. You can do this with technology such as
Plickers, which will be discussed in Chapter 5, or a Google Form.
You could ask students to circle their choice on a piece of paper
and put it in the suggestion box. You could also simply ask your
students to raise their hand for their choice.

After the votes have been tallied, you will want students to
be thoughtful in generating a list of all of the tasks that need to be
completed in order to finish the chosen service-learning project.
The tasks can be grouped by similarity. These groups can then
become departments or task groups for your students. You can
determine which student gets assigned to which group, or you
can allow them to self-assign. Each group member should have
an assigned role so that the workload is effectively distributed.

Service-learning projects provide opportunities for students
to act as problem solvers, critical thinkers, researchers, and agents
for change. There is untold value in students seeing that they can
positively affect change, and for them to see how their actions
have improved and helped address a school or community need.

Conclusion

Being able to collaborate and work well with others is an essential skill, not just for the K-12 years, but for being a productive adult as well. This chapter contains several strategies for helping students gain the necessary essential skills to engage in collaborative settings. As educators, we need to accept the challenge of providing students with the opportunity to learn these skills. All of the strategies in Chapters 1 to 4 will provide students with the skills and confidence to engage in collaborative work. In Chapter 5, we will share strategies in a scaffolded manner to get the maximum benefit of collaborative work.

Self-Reflection

1. What are some other essential skills that you consider to be necessary?
2. In what ways might you be intentional with modeling the essential skills outlined in this chapter?
3. What ideas might you have for service-learning projects?

References

Ditkowsky, A. (2018, November 1). *For educators: How to build empathy and strengthen your school community.* Retrieved February 1, 2020, from https://mcc.gse.harvard.edu/resources-for-educators/how-build-empathy-strengthen-school-community

Gordon, T. (2016). *Origins of the Gordon Model.* Retrieved January 17, 2020, from www.gordontraining.com/thomas-gordon/origins-of-the-gordon-model/

5

Collaborative Strategies for Effective Learning

Even in the most engaging and relationship-rich classrooms, you will have to work up to collaborative-learning groups. All students, regardless of their circumstances, will benefit from scaffolding engagement opportunities. This gives time to establish rapport, build connections with and among your students, and lay the foundation for a climate and culture of trust, safety, and positive relationships. As an educator, you will be more successful in getting students to participate if you have implemented some of the strategies already discussed in this book.

Mission Statement

In thinking about creating a classroom culture of learning, and as students begin to develop supportive relationships, there need to be some guiding principles in how they are going to work together to be successful (even on those bad days). A classroom mission statement can set the tone for the day-to-day interactions and how the class will function as part of its daily routine. It is imperative that students of all ages have the opportunity to have a voice in what kind of environment and interactions make them feel safe, productive, and confident.

One way to create student commitment is by turning the process of creating a mission statement over to them. If they have already experienced a process, such as the one in Chapter 3, of giving input into the development of class norms, they may be ready for a student-led affinity diagram. Younger students would likely still need teacher facilitation, but older students could easily generate questions such as "What do we need to be prepared to learn every day?", "What do I need from my teacher to learn every day?", and "How can I help my peers learn every day?" Once students have had the chance to respond on sticky notes, on index cards, or electronically, they can take the lead and sort the ideas based on similar themes. The class can then see the biggest needs for their class as learners and begin writing a brief, concise mission statement to be posted in the classroom, as a reminder for what is expected of each individual to ensure a classroom culture of learning.

A mission statement is a tool to promote positive relationships and to foster individual responsibility and effective teamwork. It is a tool that must become part of daily work habits and not just seen as a poster on the wall. An outside visitor walking into the classroom should be able to see the mission statement posted and observe its principles in action. See Figure 5.1 for an elementary example and Figure 5.2 for a middle school Social Studies example.

Once the mission statement is posted and understood, students should begin to have a feeling of safety and will more likely take risks and participate more freely. It helps provide purpose and context for student learning. Similar to norms, both teachers and students should feel comfortable with pointing out behaviors that do not support the class's stated mission.

Individual Engagement Activities

Agreement/Disagreement Emojis

A fun and relevant strategy to get students comfortable with responding in class is the agreement/disagreement emojis. These were mentioned in our Chapter 2 discussion about building connections between students. Using emoji responses

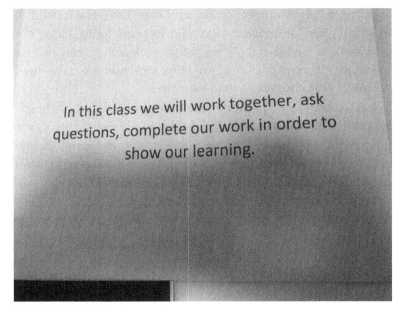

FIGURE 5.1
Elementary Classroom Mission Statement

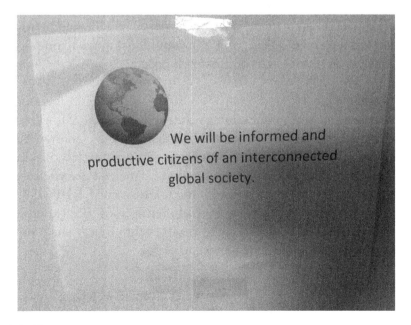

FIGURE 5.2
Middle School Social Studies Mission Statement

is easy, relatively budget friendly, and safe. Even the most timid and introverted of students are able to participate. Once your students have created their response sticks, they can be used to get a quick snapshot of where your students are, who needs more time, and who is ready to move on.

As discussed in Chapter 2, the emoji response tools help to establish rapport and connections between your students. Giving students the opportunity to respond to non-academic content can help them develop and gain confidence to respond eventually to more academic-based statements or questions.

Another emoji-based activity that can be used to gauge understanding or to do a quick class-feelings check is to give the students different emojis, such as happy, sad, confused, or angry. They can hold up whichever emoji correlates to how they are feeling that day or in response to that question. The ability to hold up a visual representation should provide a more accurate picture of what's really happening in the classroom, as students will be less likely to feel pressured to respond in a certain way.

If you feel that your students may benefit from extra movement (right after lunch or right after recess), the same activity can be done using sides of the room, or a line made from painter's tape on the floor. Students would just move to one side of the line or room based on their response.

White Boards

White boards are another strategy that you can employ to garner individual student responses. Their use isn't as anonymous as some of the other strategies discussed, but they do provide a sense of safety in that responses don't have to be verbalized. There is some cost involved with the use of white boards. If the price is prohibitive, there are some other options. For example, you can use plain sheets of paper inserted into a clear sheet protector, or you can laminate a piece of paper.

Consensogram

As mentioned in Chapter 3, another quick way to provide an opportunity for students to respond individually, and to also get a snapshot of where the class is as a whole, is the use of a

Consensogram. A Consensogram is a tool that charts where students are in their readiness with content, misconceptions they may have, or feelings they have on a given topic. Steps for utilizing this tool could be as follows:

1. Determine a topic or question for which you would like to establish some baseline data, for instructional planning or grouping purposes.

Consensogram Examples

Primary Age Example

What do you know about plants?

1	2	3
I know what they look like.	I know the names of some plants and some parts of a plant.	I know the parts of a plant and I've grown one.

FIGURE 5.3
Consensogram for Primary Students

Intermediate Age Example

How prepared do you feel for the Civil War assessment?
2/02 X   2/05 X

I still have questions and would like a teacher or peer conference.

X X X X X X X X X X X X
X X X X

I need to review my notes.

X X X X X X X X X X X X X
X X X X X X X X

I feel prepared.

X X X X

X X X X X X X X X X X X X X X X

FIGURE 5.4
Consensogram for Intermediate Students Showing Before and After

2. Create the Consensogram either on chart paper, where students can place individual stickers, or electronically, with a variety of digital tools.

3. Once students have responded, use the data either to lead a class discussion based on the results, or to adjust teaching plans and the formation of groups.

4. A Consensogram is also a valuable tool if you want to collect before and after data. Once the instruction has been adjusted and applied, students can be given a different-colored dot to indicate their shift in readiness or beliefs. See Figure 5.3 of a primary student example. See Figure 5.4 for an example for intermediate students utilizing the before and after data.

Technology Tools for Individual Responses

You can also use technology-based options for individual responses. Technology is a great way to provide anonymity of responses while ensuring that there is equitable access for all students to participate. These options are easy for students of all ages to use. Educational technology changes so quickly that it can be overwhelming to keep up. Some of our favorite tools are Plickers, Flipgrid, and Pear Deck. We will discuss these briefly here. Please be sure to check your school district's technology policies and practices before using any of these tools in your classroom.

Plickers is very similar to the Clickers system of old. To use Plickers, you create a class list and assign each student a number. Once this is done, you print out a class set of response cards. These response cards resemble QR codes. Each response card is slightly different. You create multiple-choice questions on the website www.plickers.com. There is an app that allows you to use your device's camera to scan student responses. Plickers works well for several reasons. The novelty helps teachers gain and hold students' attention. It provides safety and anonymity. Students can see how the class has answered as a whole, but not individually. Teachers do have access to that information, providing a quick, formative assessment. Plickers is an exciting way to integrate technology with your class without needing a lot of access to student technology devices.

Another alternative, if you are a 1:1 school, is to bring your own device to school or have a classroom set of devices. Here, Pear Deck might be an option. Pear Deck is an add-on for Google Slides and Microsoft PowerPoint, and allows you to create an interactive slide presentation. There are several different options for questions. Students can join a presentation using a code and can respond to the teacher's questions from their devices. Answers are anonymous, but can be displayed for the class to view. There is a premium version that allows for teacher access to a dashboard, where individual responses can be viewed. Pear Deck also allows for teachers to select templates from its library. Content areas include Math, Social Studies, world languages, and even SEL. More information is available on the Pear Deck website at www.peardeck.com.

Flipgrid (www.flipgrid.com) works much like an online message board. On this message board, called a grid, teachers can post a question or even a sentence starter. Students can respond to the prompt straight from the grid by recording videos. The videos can be created in the app or through the website. One of the advantages of Flipgrid is that teachers can turn on commenting capabilities (or not) so that students may interact with classmates.

Technology can be an incredibly powerful engagement tool. It provides anonymity, safety, and the opportunity for all students to be heard. Once students have had some experience and success with independent response strategies, you can start introducing pair, trio, or group strategies. These strategies will be shared next.

Small-Group/Partner Engagement Activities

The go-to strategies educators most frequently utilize to engage students in discourse are "Turn and Talk" or "Think-Pair-Share." These strategies are used so much for a few reasons:

1. Turn and Talk to a partner requires no movement. The student partners with someone sitting beside them and talks about the prompt.
2. There is no prep work besides including the discussion prompts in lesson planning and remembering to provide the opportunity.
3. Think-Pair-Share is similar, but you could add the extra step of movement. The student thinks about the prompt, pairs up with someone in the room, and shares their thinking.

Although both of these strategies allow for discourse and an opportunity for students to share their thinking or questions, they are often overused, leading to students not staying on topic or unprepared for higher levels of thinking. Students need to be explicitly taught how to engage in these conversations, and allowed an appropriate amount of thinking time in order to be ready to share their thinking.

The following strategies will help educators think beyond Think-Pair-Share by considering different formations of groups and utilizing less frequently used collaboration strategies. Positive relationships have been built in the learning environment and the essential skills have been taught; now let's give students the opportunity to collaborate in a variety of ways.

Forming Groups

When thinking about forming partnerships and groups, we often get stuck in how we group them. As mentioned earlier, once they have determined special interests, a teacher can tap into that information to begin forming partnerships and then eventually larger groups. The structure of the partner/group work needs to be defined. Roles and responsibilities must always be communicated. Each group member should always have some type of role to ensure accountability of all members. Random pairings could occur from a simple lineup in alphabetical order according to first name (or some other variable). You can really get creative with your lineup variables.

An engaging way to group students is to pass out an image to each student and ask them to find their "duo." The images could be common things that most of us believe go together, like eggs and bacon, peanut butter and jelly, chicken nuggets and ketchup. These pairings are likely to spark a spirited conversation about who has ever had that combination, who believes the combination is gross, and who can come up with a grosser combination. This is also a good way to pull in language for those with language deficits and limited English.

Older students may enjoy trio or quartet images that represent people in pop culture, sports figures, musical geniuses, or other familiar characters. If you choose to use pop culture references for grouping, make sure that you choose people, movies, or references that are relevant to your students. We once used this strategy during a professional development training and used movies from the 1980s. The participants in the audience were so young that we spent quite a bit of time explaining what the movies were! The possibilities are limitless on how students can be grouped, and trying new ways of grouping will engage students and promote the interaction of diverse groups that could include culture, social class, special needs, and academic readiness differences. See Tool 5.5 for pairs cards and Tool 5.6 for trio cards and a sample recording sheet.

Tool 5.5 Pairs Cards

Duo cards for younger students

Duo cards for older students

Tool 5.6 Trio Cards

Images obtained from Pexels. All photos and videos on Pexels are free for commercial use.

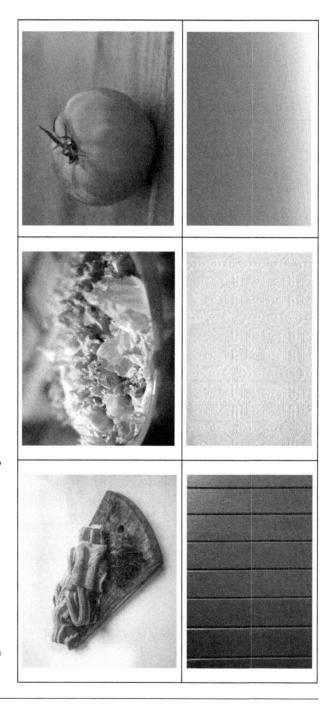

Equilateral	Obtuse	Scalene
Electron	Neuron	Proton
Ectoderm	Mesoderm	Endoderm
Sedimentary	Metamorphic	Igneous
Belmont Stakes	Preakness Stakes	Kentucky Derby

Recording Sheet

Record each group member's ideas.

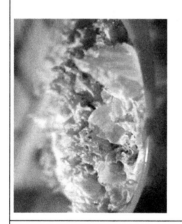

Gallery Walk

Small group/whole group: A gallery walk is an authentic opportunity for students to begin utilizing interpersonal skills described in previous chapters. This strategy can be executed in a variety of ways. One means is to have students work collaboratively to create a chart, poster, brainstorm of ideas, or visual representation of a concept – basically, any way you would like them to respond to a specific topic or prompt. Once groups are formed, the workload is divided among the members. Suggested roles may be recorder (charts information), illustrator (draws on concept), timekeeper/facilitator (to keep the group on track), and reporter (who is going to share with the class). Other roles could be assigned or shared.

Once each group has had time to create their poster, the charts are hung around the room or in a hallway. The group may be given a rubric, a checklist, a graphic organizer, or some type of note-taking tool, and the groups rotate around the gallery to see the rest of the class's work. A time could be set to indicate time to rotate. Older students may be given the option to complete the gallery walk in a designated time (15 minutes) and then return to their seats. Another variation of the gallery walk is for the groups to rotate sticky notes and pencils and share feedback with each group by recording an affirmation or question on their work. The final step of the gallery walk may be to get each group to review their feedback and make adjustments, and then the reporter can share out to the rest of the class. The gallery walk can be an effective way for students to practice critical-thinking skills, interpersonal skills, and speaking and listening skills. See Figure 5.7 for an example of a primary gallery walk example.

Agreement Thermometer

Whole group leading to small group: One activity to promote movement is to create a human thermometer. After being given a topic or question, where a student stands on the thermometer indicates their level of agreement. In order to place themselves

Gallery Walk Example

Pieces of chart paper are posted around the room with a different question, topic, or idea on each for students to respond. Students can respond either with a writing utensil or written response on sticky note. Responses can be constructed by individuals, pairs, or groups.

Long a sound	Short a sound
	cat
tape	
same	hat
hate	ran
	pan
came	tag
	Sam

Students could also have the option of drawing pictures or choosing words on cards to sort on the charts. After the lists have been generated, students could take turns going to the charts and deciding whether they agree or disagree with the placement of the words.

FIGURE 5.7
Primary Gallery Walk Example

on the spectrum, they must be ready to explain their reasoning. The agreement thermometer could be labeled with painter's tape on the floor or it could be an imaginary line with designated points. Once students have made their stance, they could then have a discussion with someone standing beside them and share their reasoning for where they are standing. Again, this is another simple activity that promotes discourse (which could lead to making a connection with a peer), perspective taking, and rapport building.

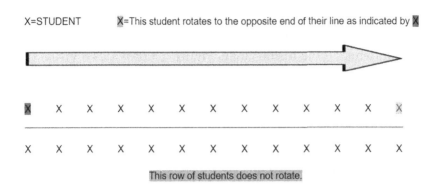

X=STUDENT   X=This student rotates to the opposite end of their line as indicated by X

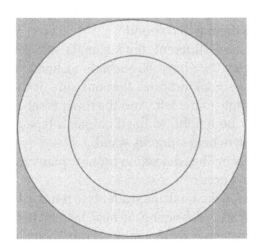

FIGURE 5.8
Speed Chatting

Speed Chatting

Whole group/partner: Speed chatting is definitely an activity that needs to be attempted only after the essential communication skills have been taught and practiced. Speed chatting requires not only listening skills, but also following directions (which may be a challenge in itself). Students can either be lined up in two parallel lines facing each other, or in two concentric circles where the students on the outside of the circle are facing the students on the inside circle. Figure 5.8 provides a visual of what this might look like.

Once students have been lined up, the speed chatting begins. Below are some suggested directions:

1. Determine topic and prompt for which you would like students to respond.
2. Tell students that they are going to share their ideas in a very short amount of time, so they need to be concise with their response. Give students time to think and if students need the added support, have them write their response to take with them.
3. Explain that once the time begins, the designated side of the lines or circles will share first, and then the person facing them will respond.
4. Have two different time signals set. The first signal indicates they have 30 seconds to finish their chat. The second signal indicates that one side of the line or circle will rotate to the left. And the timer is set again.
5. It may be helpful to have painter's tape on the floor to indicate where students stand.
6. The teacher has discretion for how many rounds of speed chatting occur.
7. When finished, ask the students to return to their seats and then lead a debriefing of new information or questions they may have experienced during their chats.
8. Students with disabilities or limited English may benefit from participating with a partner. Students that need additional think time, are shy, or lack confidence may benefit from having a partner to discuss the prompt with before lining up.

Fishbowl

Whole group to model small group: The fishbowl is another way to promote student discussions. It may be a good idea to model the strategy with a small group before having groups attempt independently. This strategy is also good to use with younger students to model what group work should look like. For older students, the same is true, but it also demonstrates the type of conversations that should occur.

The premise is a small group sits in a circle facing each other. Discourse begins based on their predetermined roles. Some teachers choose to give students "talking chips" to ensure balanced participation in the group.

The rest of the class stands in a circle around the group with a checklist, a rubric, or a Plus/Delta to provide feedback to the group, based on their interactions and expectations for group work.

When students have gained independence with group work, you can vary the directions and the goal of each group. The outside circle could be composed of another small group who do not record notes about the interaction of the group, but who take notes on the content of the conversations.

Expanding Groups

Whole group/small group: As the name implies, this activity starts small and expands, meaning the group gets larger. Any type of prompt can be given for this activity. It could be a response to a selected reading, a discussion question for a video, an opinion, or a review. It's simply a way for students to reflect on content individually, then to share their thinking and hear the thinking of others to come to a conclusion.

1. Provide a prompt to students that will elicit a response.
2. Give students think time, then ask them to respond in writing.
3. Students then pair up with another student based on your directions; for example, someone who has the same color shirt as them.
4. The partners share their ideas, then determine one most important point based on both of their responses.
5. The partners now team up with another set of partners, creating a quartet. Each set of partners shares their most

important idea. They will then use both of their ideas to expand on one most important idea.

6. When complete, create an affinity diagram so students can analyze the responses as a class.

With regard to duo and trio cards mentioned previously, this activity lends itself to using famous or recognizable groups of four, such as seasons of the year. Partners can easily identify at least one other person to be a partner, leaving two others available to be partners, then in the last step they become four. Having the directions for the expanding groups visible would be beneficial and helpful for students that have difficulty following multistep directions.

Conversation Stations

Small group: Conversation stations are similar to speed chatting, except students work in small groups. Prompts are placed at tables or areas around the room. Students work together to complete the assigned task and complete a recording sheet to document their work and participation.

The size of the class will determine how many conversation stations to plan. It's recommended to have no more than four students per station. See Tool 5.9 for an example of how this could look.

Tool 5.9 Conversation Stations

Math Examples

Each table or station would have a different prompt and recording sheet related to a topic.

Students work together to complete. Each station should also have mathematical-language frames to help guide the discussion and reinforce vocabulary. The size of the class will determine how many conversation stations to plan. Recommended no more than four per station.

Elementary

Chat Station #1 Discuss the problem. Choose a strategy. Solve the problem. Choose a different strategy to check your answer.
Aiden went to ten houses on his street for Halloween. Five of the houses gave him a sucker. What fraction of houses on Aiden's street gave him a sucker?

Chat Station #2 Discuss the problem. Choose a strategy. Solve the problem. Choose a different strategy to check your answer.
Taylor is painting a portrait of her best friend, Lisa. To make it easier, she divides the portrait into six equal parts. What fraction represents each part of the portrait?

I agree/disagree with you because…
What key words helped you solve this?
Can you explain this to me?
What were you thinking here?
How did you solve it?
Why did you choose that operation?
What strategy did you use?
Why did you choose that strategy?
How did you know your answer was right?
How else can you solve it?

Secondary

Chat Station #1
Kristen and Connor were walking their dog Ruby in the neighborhood.
Connor walks at 5 km/h, and is just behind Kristen, who walks at 6 km/h.
Ruby runs from boy to girl and back again with a constant speed of 10 km/h. Ruby does not slow down on the turn.
How far does Ruby travel in 1 hour?

Chat Station #2
David took a trip to see a friend. His friend lives 225 miles away. He drove in town at an average speed of 30 mph, then he drove on the interstate at an average speed of 70 mph. The trip took three-and-a-half hours, total. How far did David drive on the interstate?

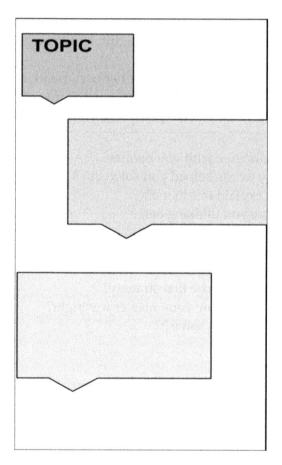

FIGURE 5.10
Text-Message Template

Text-Message Responses

Small group: Although the name implies technology, this activity does not require technology at all! Print out an image of a smartphone screen, or you can challenge your students to draw one. Then get students to respond to a prompt by creating a series of emojis to communicate their understanding or a question they may have. This is a very engaging task for all ages (even adults!) because it takes away the fear of misspelling words or not using correct grammar. See Figure 5.10 for a text-message template.

Conclusion

Multiple strategies have been shared in this chapter to help students gain the confidence needed to participate in collaborative settings. We know that once students feel like they are part of a school community, they are more likely to take chances with their learning.

All of the strategies and activities described within the scope of each chapter are aligned with John Hattie's most recent update of the *250+ influences on student achievement* report (Visible Learning, 2017), which indicates how cooperative learning, communication skills, positive peer influences, and small-group learning have substantial effect sizes that impact the learning of our students.

Self-Reflection

1. Thinking about your current student roster, which strategies would you like to use with them?
2. How might you leverage technology or other novel engagement techniques to capture your students' interest?
3. How will implementing some of the strategies throughout this book impact your students' learning?

Reference

Visible Learning (2017). *250+ influences on student achievement.* Retrieved November 15, 2019, from https://visible-learning.org/wp-content/uploads/2018/03/VLPLUS-252-Influences-Hattie-ranking-DEC-2017.pdf

6

What to Do When Things Don't Go as Planned

Classroom mission statement created with students ✓
Norms established ✓
Routines practiced ✓
Anchor chart visual reminders posted ✓

What could go wrong? Plenty. Even the best-made plans and the most supportive, safe, and connected classrooms should anticipate disruption of some sort. Below are situations that might hinder the effectiveness of student collaboration. We've also included some troubleshooting ideas to consider.

Off-Task Behavior

One of the biggest concerns that teachers have with students working in small groups is a management issue. What about those students who are not doing what they are supposed to be doing? Even with the best classroom management, there will be times when students are off task. Assigning roles for the group and having one person as a monitor is one option. Using a group rubric to assess the work performance is another option. Healthy competition could also be a motivator. For being on task and completing work, groups could earn points toward a class-chosen privilege, such as being able to line up first for lunch or recess. Older students may be motivated by homework passes or extra screen time. A common goal can be very motivating for a group, and it encourages self-monitoring behavior for the good of the group.

Educators also need to be aware that what appears to be off-task behavior may be an indication of something else. That student staring off into the distance, or with their head on their desk, may need processing time to complete the next task or recall directions. Students affected by trauma or living in poverty may need additional reminders regarding the steps in the task, or a visual of steps that need to be taken in order to participate in the group. "Think time" may look different from student to student. This is yet another reason that building relationships and knowing your students is so important. Knowing the background of your students will allow you to provide additional support without accidentally violating a student's boundary or triggering their stress-response system.

Accountability

There is a misconception that every task completed in a small group needs to have a product. Students can be held accountable without turning in a piece of paper. Teachers do not need another piece of paper to stick in their teacher bag that may or may not be graded. As mentioned before, a group rubric for the day's participation can be completed and turned in by the group. When creating a rubric for collaborative work, it may be helpful to model examples and non-examples of indicators on the rubric for younger students. Tool 6.1 is an example of a group-work accountability rubric.

Tool 6.1   Group Accountability Rubric

Group-Work Rubric Examples

Including the class in creating a rubric for group expectations is a useful way to reinforce the class mission statement. Below are a few examples.

Novice	Apprentice	Proficient	Distinguished
• Contributed very little to the group's project. • Needed to be begged to focus and produce. • Frequently off task. • Distracted group. • Did not complete his or her share.	• Contributed good effort to the group's project. • Was helpful and cooperative in completing his or her share.	• Contributed great effort to the group's project. • Did a good job of organizing group efforts and keeping people on track. • Completed his or her share with great effort.	• Contributed exceptional effort to the group's project. • Did a fantastic job in organizing group efforts and keeping people on track. • Went above and beyond the call of duty to further group's work.
Rarely provides useful ideas when participating in the group and in classroom discussion.	Sometimes provides useful ideas when participating in the group and in classroom discussion.	Usually provides useful ideas when participating in the group and in classroom discussion.	Routinely provides useful ideas when participating in the group and in classroom discussion.
May refuse to participate.	A satisfactory group member who does what is required.	A strong group member who tries hard!	A leader who contributes a lot of effort.

Accountability for older students might look a little different. Students could develop contracts on what tasks each group member will complete and what the reasonable consequence would be if the contract is not upheld by a group member. The consequence could be attached to a reduction in the individual's grade for the work, or added workload. This would be more appropriate for a project-based assignment or long-term collaboration.

Another idea to promote accountability in collaborative groups is to have students "apply" for different roles in the group and, as a group, determine who is best suited for each task. This would require a high level of essential skills for group members, and lots of prior opportunities to work collaboratively in different groups.

Heterogeneous Abilities

Planning for mixed-ability groups can be a challenge. Although it may seem ideal to have students with varying levels of skills, the roles that are assigned to the group members need to be appropriate for their independent working level. With that being said, this does not mean that higher-performing students get more challenging tasks or more of the workload.

Students with disabilities and English-language learners need to be given tasks that are appropriate for their learning needs, and they need to be provided with appropriate, specially designed instruction. By intentionally focusing on building peer and classroom relationships, students should have the opportunity for perspective taking and to realize that work assignments are intended to be equitable, not equal. Many times, students are accustomed to working in homogeneous ability groups where the expectations are the same for each group member. Are we stifling or fostering a fixed mindset with some of our struggling students by not providing them with opportunities to work with higher-performing students? Those same higher-performing students can also benefit from collaborating with students of different abilities.

Absent Students

Student absenteeism in most cases will be inevitable. Teachers should have a routine in place for students who are absent from a group task. Being absent does not necessarily mean not being at school. Students may not be present for other reasons that include intervention pull-out, counseling sessions, or various other unanticipated reasons.

Although students may be required to work collaboratively, a system needs to be in place, so the absence of a group member does not deter the work of the rest of the group. This can be done by assigning tasks to individuals that are not dependent upon the work of others. Another strategy could be to assign two students to one task, so the work can still be done, which the absent member can complete upon return.

Many classrooms have moved to digital platforms that allow students to collaborate without being in the same room or space. This would be a possible option for students to complete group work when absent. We have seen more and more virtual collaboration across grade levels in recent months and can assume this will become a trend, not only in education, but throughout today's workforce.

Personality Conflicts

Oil and water. It's going to happen. We all know there are going to be times when students just don't get along. To be honest, there may be times when there is a personality conflict between teacher and student. Again, it goes back to relationships. This is when you might want to return to Chapter 1 and apply the strategies you started using to maintain boundaries and to deal with button pushers. We need to model both of those for our students. Without purposefully pointing out when you are doing it, students will still take notice of your interactions with their peers, especially the most difficult ones. By not calling explicit attention to your use of strategies, you provide a great opportunity for your students to see you model grace.

Although it may be easiest to just not partner or group conflicting personalities together, students need to understand that throughout our lives there are going to be times when we just don't get along with someone, or we just don't click. Learning to collaborate with others who may be very different from us is a life skill. When we enter the workforce there will be a boss, a coworker, even future family members that we may not agree with, but we must collaborate. When this occurs in the classroom it would be best to have a one-on-one conference with each student to determine a root cause. A next step would be to establish a set of norms for the two when working together.

That ONE Student

We've all had him/her at some point in our careers. That ONE student who just flat out refuses to participate or purposely disrupts small groups or independent work. That one student who pushes all of your buttons – even the ones you didn't know you had. That one student may be living with the effects of growing up in generational poverty; she might be a victim of trauma; he may have been displaced from his home unexpectedly. That one student is the one who probably does not have many, if any, positive, healthy relationships. That one student is the one that you may have a hard time developing a relationship with, but for someone else, it may come more easily. For difficult students, it's imperative that we identify the hidden strengths they bring with them every day. What do they value? What motivates them – are they even able to articulate this? If they aren't able to articulate what motivates them, you may need to spend some time helping them discover it. Establishing connectedness is key to getting buy-in with these individuals. After conferencing with the student, to not necessarily find the root of the behavior, but to seek a compromise or a solution to the disruptions, one option would be to create a contract of expectations, outcomes, and consequences that are mutually acceptable. Students want to share their voice, and educators are in the position to help close the gap between students' needs/wants and what is acceptable in the learning environment. Another option would be to scaffold learning experiences from independent, to partner, then small group, based on a set of behavioral criteria for each collaborative formation. No matter what strategy you decide to use with that ONE student, make sure it's addressed privately with the student. Embarrassing or humiliating the student in front of classmates will only make things worse.

Final Thoughts on Troubleshooting

- ◆ Consistency in routines and expectations are key to effective student collaboration.
- ◆ The class mission statement should be the focus of the learning environment; emphasizing this is our purpose and that these principles are the ways we will reach our goals.
- ◆ Scaffolding is important to explicitly teach students how to respond in different situations. Many opportunities to work with a partner need to be experienced before students move into student-led small groups.
- ◆ Whole-group strategies such as the fishbowl can be utilized to demonstrate expectations of different roles that may be assigned to a group.
- ◆ Offer the class the opportunity to choose from different collaborative strategies. Complete a Plus/Delta at the end of the session to identify if students were engaged and if the grouping helped their learning, or whether changes

could be made in the routine to make the strategy more effective. This is important because students may collectively enjoy a specific strategy, but if their learning outcomes are not improving, another strategy needs to be utilized or modified.

◆ Intentional planning of collaborative strategies is a necessity to ensure an effective experience. Routines need to be thought through, explicitly taught, practiced, and posted as a visual reminder. These routines will likely need to be revisited after long breaks from school.

◆ Engagement strategies should be included in lesson planning. The lesson plans should also reflect specific needs of students, such as specially designed instruction, vocabulary barriers, and behavior considerations. Tool 6.2 shows a blank sample elementary engagement plan and Tool 6.3 shows a completed elementary engagement plan. Tool 6.4 shows a blank secondary engagement plan and Tool 6.5 shows a completed secondary engagement plan.

Tool 6.2 Elementary Engagement Plan

Student Engagement Lesson Plan

Date:	
Lesson:	
Standard(s) Addressed:	

Independent Response Techniques	**Materials/Technology Needed**
Paired Response Techniques	**Materials/Technology Needed**
Small-Group Techniques	**Materials/Technology Needed**
Whole-Group Techniques	**Materials/Technology Needed**

Post-Lesson Reflection:

What worked well?
What could I have done differently?
How can I improve student engagement next time?
On a scale of 1–10, with a 1 being horrible, and a 10 being fantastic, how would you rate the effectiveness of this engagement plan?

Tool 6.3 Completed Elementary Engagement Plan

Student Engagement Lesson Plan

Elementary

Date: *09-06*

Lesson: *5th Grade Social Studies*

1. *Students will make a list of responsibilities they have at home, in school, and in their community on Pear Deck slide.*

2. *Review the following freedoms/rights: expression, religion, voting, equal treatment, fair treatment by the government. Have students predict/list one responsibility they believe goes with each right.*

3. *Assign five groups based on the above rights.*

4. *Each group will then analyze the given scenarios and determine what responsibilities are connected to their assigned "right." Scenarios will be leveled according to independent reading level.*

5. *Groups will choose one scenario to share with the class.*

6. *During the presentations, students will record on a chart whether they agree or disagree with the opinion presented. Students will then have to validate their opinion with an explanation when called upon.*

The following summative assessment will be given in ORQ response:

1. *Choose one responsibility that you have at home and school and describe how you demonstrate responsibility at both places.*

2. *Describe one right you have as a US citizen and what responsibility do you have because of that freedom.*

*Readers and scribe provided based on IEPs.

Standard(s) Addressed:

SS-5-GC-U-5: as members of a democratic society, all citizens of the United States have certain rights and responsibilities, including civic participation.

Independent Response Techniques	Materials/ Technology Needed
Students will list responsibilities they have at home, at school, and in their community.	*Pear Deck slide* My Responsibilities Home: School: Community: *Assistive technology as identified on IEPs.*

Paired Response Techniques	Materials/ Technology Needed
Use pairs cards to partner students. On white/dry-erase boards, pairs will list one responsibility that goes with each right/freedom.	*Pairs cards White/dry-erase boards/ marker/eraser Visual model* *Right/responsibility: Expression Religion Voting Equal treatment Fair government*
Small-Group Techniques	Materials/Technology Needed
Expanding groups: Each pair will get with another pair based on proximity.	*Scenario cards*
Whole-Group Techniques	Materials/ Technology Needed
Review five freedoms/rights: Expression Religion Voting Equal treatment Fair government *Each group will share one scenario.*	*Google slideshow* *Agree/Disagree cards*

Post-Lesson Reflection:

What worked well? *The pacing of the lesson and transitions from whole-group/partner/independent activities*

What could I have done differently? *Be more strategic when passing out pairs cards to minimize off-task behavior*

How can I improve student engagement next time? *Be more intentional about monitoring the expanding groups and give feedback to each group*

On a scale of 1–10, with a 1 being horrible, and a 10 being fantastic, how would you rate the effectiveness of this engagement plan? *8*

Tool 6.4   Secondary Engagement Plan

Student Engagement Lesson Plan

Date:	Period:
Lesson:	
Standard(s) Addressed:	
Independent Response Techniques	Materials/Technology Needed
Paired Response Techniques	Materials/Technology Needed

Small-Group Techniques	Materials/Technology Needed
Whole-Group Techniques	Materials/Technology Needed

Post-Lesson Reflection:

What worked well?

What could I have done differently?

How can I improve student engagement next time?

On a scale of 1–10, with a 1 being horrible, and a 10 being fantastic, how would you rate the effectiveness of this engagement plan?

Tool 6.5 Completed Secondary Engagement Plan

Student Engagement Lesson Plan

Secondary

Date: *03-15-03/3–19*

Lesson: *Setting, Point of View, Plot – What If?* *(week-long plan)*

1. *Students will be asked to brainstorm a list of their favorite movies or television shows.*
2. *Ask students to choose two from their list; after think time, ask students to write a description of a setting in both of their picks.*

3. *Ask students to choose one movie or show. Have class line up in alphabetical order according to the name of their choice.*
4. *Once students have shared, ask them to number off by ones, twos, and fours in the order they are standing (this may change based on number in attendance).*
5. *Once students know their number, form small groups.*
6. *In each small group, assign roles: recorder, artist, reporter, facilitator, timekeeper (some roles may need to be shared).*
7. *Group members will share their favorite movie/show and describe the setting. For each of the settings, the group will discuss possibilities of "What if?" the setting was different. How would that impact the characters in the movie/show? How might the plot be impacted? Groups will create a chart to share with the class to demonstrate how each of their movies/shows would be impacted if it occurred in a different setting. Share out.*
8. *Students will independently complete an exit slip to describe how a change in setting could impact the characters or plot.*

9. *These same steps will be followed by choosing different movies/shows from their brainstormed list for Point of View and Plot. Five days expected to complete.*

*Scribe or assistive technology for students x, y, z
*Pay attention to where students a, b, c, d line up.
*Check in with student E during small-group time to check behavior-tracker sheet

Standard(s) Addressed:

CCSS.ELA-LITERACY.RL.7.3
Analyze how particular elements of a story or drama
interact (e.g. how setting shapes the characters or plot).

Independent Response Techniques	Materials/Technology Needed
Students will individually complete the exit slip.	*Exit slip* *"In your own words, describe how a change in setting can impact other elements such as character and plot."*
Paired Response Techniques	Materials/Technology Needed
Small-Group Techniques	Materials/Technology Needed
Assign roles: recorder, artist, reporter, facilitator, timekeeper.	*Chart paper* *Drawing tools* *Timer*
Whole-Group Techniques	Materials/Technology Needed
Independent brainstorm. *Human Number Line – line up in alphabetical order according to title.*	*Graphic organizer for brainstorming* *Quick write*

Post-Lesson Reflection:

What worked well?

What could I have done differently?

How can I improve student engagement next time?

On a scale of 1–10, with a 1 being horrible, and a 10 being fantastic, how would you rate the effectiveness of this engagement plan?

Conclusion

Relationship building is an absolutely necessary skill as an adult. Providing opportunities for students to work in collaborative settings with a variety of peers now is good practice for what will happen in the future. It gives students ample time to practice essential skills that will make them more marketable in an ever-changing workforce. Being a good team member is a skill that most employers prefer (Adams, 2015) and will help students stand out when looking for employment. Eventually, classmates become colleagues. Practicing with collaboration also gives students valuable insight into how they work best in a group, what their boundaries are, and what behaviors may push their buttons. This also gives students ample time to develop coping strategies for when they are forced to work with colleagues who violate their boundaries or push their buttons for whatever reason.

Self-Reflection

1. Rate yourself: On a scale of 1 to 4, where are you regarding readiness to be more intentional with planning and implementing collaborative strategies beyond Think-Pair-Share (see Table 6.6)?

TABLE 6.6 Rate Yourself

1	2	3	4
My focus needs to be on creating a classroom environment of learning, to support collaborative strategies.	I still need to work on structured partner expectations, then I will be ready to choose a collaborative strategy.	I'm ready. I've chosen one or two strategies that I want to begin using.	I've got this! I'm already thinking about how to modify a few strategies to make them my own.

2. What are your next steps to implementing collaborative learning in your classroom/setting?

Reference

Adams, S. (2015, February 19). *The 10 skills employers most want in 20-something employees*. Retrieved April 3, 2020, from www.forbes.com/sites/susanadams/2013/10/11/the-10-skills-employers-most-want-in-20-something-employees/#7f8d3f476330

Appendix A: Strategies at a Glance

This is a list of the strategies explored in each of the chapters in this book.

Chapter 1: How Do You Do It? Building Connections *with* Students

Establishing boundaries
Knowing what pushes your buttons
Building rapport

>Smiling
>Using students' preferred names

Gathering student expectations of what teacher behaviors will help them learn
Suggestion box
Biopoems
Finding hidden strengths
Warm demander

Chapter 2: How Do You Do It? Building Connections *between* Students

Hey, Me Too!
Would You Rather?
Identifying special interests and hobbies

Classroom bingo
Class calendar
Student partnerships
Seating arrangements

Chapter 3: Laying the Foundation for Collaborative Learning

Classroom norms
    Consensogram – commitment to norms
Class meetings

Chapter 4: Making Sure Your Students Have the Necessary Essential Skills

Active listening
Academic language
Sentence stems
    Paraphrasing
Disagreeing politely
Being a productive team member
Perspective taking
Empathy

Chapter 5: Collaborative Strategies for Effective Learning

Mission statement
    Affinity diagram
Agreement/disagreement emojis
White boards
Consensogram
Plickers
Pear Deck
Flipgrid
Forming groups
    Duo/trio/quartet cards

Gallery walk
Agreement thermometer
Speed chatting
Fishbowl
Expanding groups
Conversation stations
Text-message responses

Chapter 6: What to Do When Things Don't Go as Planned

The strategies listed below will help with problem solving class-room issues.

Revisit class mission statement
Scaffold engagement
Use whole group to model
Offer choice in engagement type
Plus/Delta feedback on engagement
Intentional teaching of routines
Intentionally include engagement in lesson plans

Appendix B: Additional Resources

These are resources that we like to share with other educators. We use these resources often in our own teaching and helping practices.

Books

Craig, S.E. (20 08). *Reaching and teaching children who hurt: Strategies for your classroom*. Baltimore, MD: Paul H. Brookes Pub.

This book has several strategies on how to teach children who've been affected by trauma and/or chronic stress. It also shares information on how the brain is affected by trauma exposure and stress.

Flerx, V.C. (2009). *Class meetings that matter: A year's worth of resources for grades K-5*. Center City, MN: Hazelden.

This resource provides a year's worth of class-meeting lessons. It helps reduce the fear in implementing something that seems a little touchy-feely. This resource is for K-5. Please note that the first few lessons address bullying as it is an Olweus Bullying Prevention Program resource.

Flerx, V.C., Limber, S., Mullin, N., Riese, J., Snyder, M., & Olweus, D. (2009). *Class meetings that matter: A year's worth of resources for grades 6–8*. Center City, MN: Hazelden.

This resource provides a year's worth of class-meeting lessons. It helps reduce the fear in implementing something that seems a little touchy-feely. This resource is for grades 6–8. Please note that the first few lessons address bullying as it is an Olweus Bullying Prevention Program resource.

Murphy, J.J. (2013). *Conducting student-driven interviews: Practical strategies for increasing student involvement and addressing behavior problems*. New York: Routledge.

This book provides information on how to use a strengths-based approach when dealing with students. Practical strategies are used to help educators find resources that are inherent in the student.

Payne, R.K. (2018). *Emotional poverty in all demographics: How to reduce anger, anxiety and violence in the classroom*. Moorabbin, Australia: Hawker Brownlow Education.

Dr. Payne's newest book introduces the term "emotional poverty." Strategies are shared that help provide students a sense of safety and belonging. There is also some background information included on Erikson's stages of development for those of us who could use a refresher.

Snyder, J.M. (2012). *Class meetings that matter: A year's worth of resources for grades 9–12*. Center City, MN: Hazelden.

This resource provides a year's worth of class-meeting lessons. It helps reduce the fear in implementing something that seems a little touchy-feely. This resource is for grades 9–12. Please note that the first few lessons address bullying as it is an Olweus Bullying Prevention Program resource.

Souers, K. & Hall, P.A. (2016). *Fostering resilient learners: Strategies for creating a trauma-sensitive classroom*. Moorabbin, Australia: Hawker Brownlow Education.

The strategies that are shared in this book are easy to implement and easy to understand. There are also some case examples that help to illustrate the authors' point.

Sousa, D.A. (2016). *Engaging the rewired brain*. Moorabbin, Australia: Hawker Brownlow Education.

This book addresses how technology has affected our students' brains. The book also provides strategies on how to leverage technology and other engagement strategies in our teaching practices.

Zacarian, D., Alvarez-Ortiz, L., & Haynes, J. (2017). *Teaching to strengths: Supporting students living with trauma, violence, and chronic stress.* Alexandria, VA: ASCD.

This resource is extremely helpful. The authors give a quick overview of trauma and its impact and then provide strategies and information on how to help students in your classroom.

Websites

The Annie E. Casey Foundation Kids Count Data Center: www.datacenter.kidscount.org

This website provides several different data points you can use to learn more about the demographics and characteristics of your community.

CASEL (The Collaborative for Academic, Social, and Emotional Learning): https://casel.org/resources/

The CASEL website provides resources and implementation tools in both the practice and research of SEL. The website will allow you to search by resource type as well as to quickly access help.

Edutopia: www.edutopia.org

Edutopia is published by the George Lucas Educational Foundation. It provides articles, resources, and strategies for classroom educators. The strategies are easy to implement.

IRIS Center: https://iris.peabody.vanderbilt.edu/resources/iris-resource-locator/

The IRIS Center provides resources and professional learning modules for educators in a range of topics.

National Child Traumatic Stress Network: www.nctsn.org

The National Child Traumatic Stress Network has several resources for people working with students or families who have been affected by trauma.

Pixabay: www.pixabay.com

Pixabay is a website with copyright-free images and videos.

The Teacher Toolkit: www.theteachertoolkit.com

This website provides teachers with resources for classroom strategies. Videos are also provided of specific strategies in action.

Materials

Chat Pack cards: https://chatpack.myshopify.com/products/

We use these Chat Pack cards a lot in our various trainings. They are really helpful for practicing active listening and paraphrasing, and can help with perspective taking. The prompts are non-academic in nature, so they are also good for making connections and building rapport.

Printed in the United States
By Bookmasters